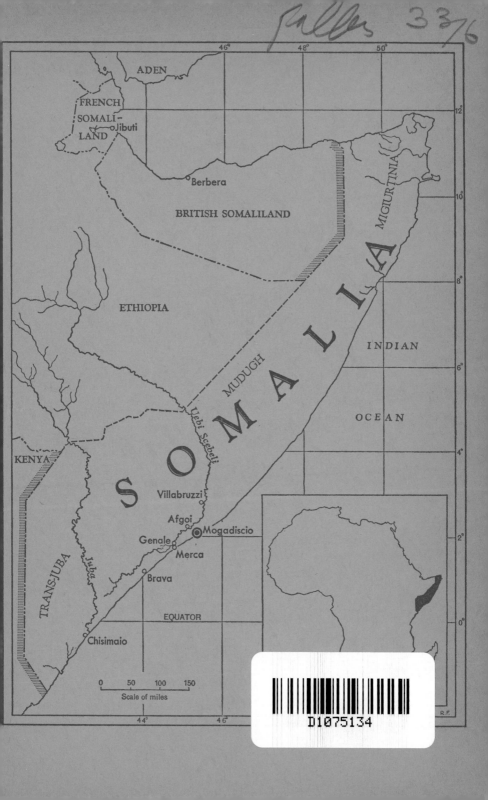

ADEN

46° 48° 50°

FRENCH
SOMALI-
LAND Jibuti

12°

Berbera

10°

BRITISH SOMALILAND

MIGIURTINIA

8°

ETHIOPIA

INDIAN

6°

MUDUGH

S O M A L I A

Uebi scebeli

OCEAN

4°

KENYA

Villabruzzi

Afgoi

2°

Genale Mogadiscio

Merca

TRANSJUBA

Juba

Brava

EQUATOR

0°

Chisimaio

0   50   100   150
Scale of miles

44° 46°

R. F.

BOSTON UNIVERSITY
African Research Studies
NUMBER 2

THE ECONOMICS OF TRUSTEESHIP IN SOMALIA

&&&

Mark Karp

AFRICAN STUDIES PROGRAM
BOSTON UNIVERSITY

Boston University Press

1 9 6 0

© 1960 by Boston University
Library of Congress Catalog Card Number: 60-11740
Manufactured in the United States of America
B. U. 7–60

Distributed by
Associated College Presses
32 Washington Place, New York 3

Preface

————— ⟨◇⟩ —————

THIS BOOK GREW out of a doctoral dissertation presented at the Fletcher School of Law and Diplomacy. It is a case study of the economic problems to which anticolonialism, in its present form, can and often does give rise in Africa. Though it is primarily addressed to economists, an effort has been made to render it accessible to students in other fields of social science who may be interested in African affairs. Technical language has therefore been kept at a minimum.

The preparation of the book required a considerable amount of research in the United States, Italy, and Somalia. It also necessitated brief visits to France and Spain. In all these countries I received much invaluable aid from many people, though, of course, I alone am responsible for the opinions expressed in this book. The list of officials, scholars, and businessmen who helped me by providing information and advice is so long that space limitations will unfortunately not permit me to thank them all individually here. I wish, however, to express particular gratitude to Professor Armando Maugini, Director of the *Istituto Agronomico per l'Oltremare* in Florence, and to Dr. Quirino Maffi of the *Istituto Italiano per l'Africa* in Rome, for their gracious hospitality and innumerable courtesies; and to Professor George N. Halm of the Fletcher School of Law and Diplomacy for having first called

to my attention an article by E. Böhm-Bawerk which provided
the theoretical keynote of this book.

Mark Karp

African Studies Program
Boston University

Contents

PREFACE   v

I Introduction   1

POLITICS AND ECONOMICS IN AFRICA   1
THE EXPERIMENT IN SOMALIA   11
ORGANIZATION OF THE BOOK   17

II The Problem of Somali Statistics   19

POPULATION   21
RESOURCES   31
NATIONAL AND PER CAPITA INCOME   34
PUBLIC FINANCE AND INTERNATIONAL PAYMENTS   35
STATISTICS AND ECONOMIC DEVELOPMENT   36

III The Pastoral Economy   38

THE LOW LEVEL OF COMMERCIALIZATION   40
THE ACCUMULATION OF LIVESTOCK   49
THE THEORY OF THE CATTLE COMPLEX   52
CRITICISM OF THE THEORY   61
THE PRECAUTIONARY MOTIVE IN HOARDING LIVESTOCK   64
THE OBSTACLES TO STRUCTURAL CHANGE   70

vii

IV *Indigenous Agriculture*   79

    UNDER-UTILIZATION OF LAND   80
    FARMER INDEBTEDNESS   83

V *The Plantation Economy*   87

    THE PRODUCTION OF BANANAS UNDER MONOPSO-
    NISTIC INFLUENCE   87
    THE PRODUCTION OF COTTON UNDER UNSTABLE
    CONDITIONS   104
    THE PRODUCTION OF SUGAR FOR DOMESTIC CONSUMP-
    TION   106

VI *The Structure of the Somali Economy as a Whole*   113

    INTERSECTORAL RELATIONS   113
    THE SCARCITY OF LABOR   117
    THE HIGH COST OF TRANSFER   121
    THE IMPORTANCE OF FOREIGN DEMAND   121

VII *The Prospects of Development*   123

    THE SEVEN YEAR PLAN   123
    EVALUATION OF THE PLAN   131
    THE SOMALI CREDIT INSTITUTE   140
    ALTERNATIVE APPROACHES   144

VIII *The Problem of Financial Dependence*   146

    THE PUBLIC BUDGET   146
    THE BALANCE OF PAYMENTS   149
    THE BANANA TRADE AND ITALIAN SUBSIDIES   154
    THE ROLE OF MONETARY POLICY   159
    THE CONCEPT OF FINANCIAL DEPENDENCE   165

IX *The Significance of the Experiment in
    Somalia*   170

  AN ECONOMIC POLICY FOR SOMALIA   172
  ECONOMIC FACTORS AND POLITICAL CHANGE   174
  APPENDIX. A NOTE ON SOME IMPLICATIONS OF THE
  EUROPEAN COMMON MARKET   178

Index   181

CHARTS

1 Fluctuations in Somalia's Cotton Exports   106
2 Domestic Output and Imports of Sugar   111
3 Fluctuations in Banana Exports and Sugar Consumption 112

TABLES

1   Population of Somalia   22
2   Ethnic Distribution of the Population, Excluding Italians
    and Aliens   23
3   Asian Population of Somalia   23
4   Percentage Distribution of the Somali Population Ac-
    cording to Occupation   24
5   Percentage Distribution of the Somali Population Ac-
    cording to Mode of Living   25
6   Population Density of Somalia, Excluding Italians and
    Aliens, 1953   26
7   Possible Annual Rates of Change of the Somali Popula-
    tion for 1931–1953   28
8   Estimates of Livestock Population   32
9   Land Distribution According to Potential Use   32
10 Area and Production of Principal Crops   33
11 National and Per Capita Income of Somalia   34

12 Role of Livestock and Livestock Products in Somalia's
    Export Trade   48
13 Relative Importance of Producers' Associations in the
    Production and Export of Bananas, 1955   89
14 Average Cost of Somali Bananas per Ton Exported, 1955   92
15 Per Capita Consumption, Expressed in Lbs., of Bananas,
    Oranges, and Tangerines in France, Italy, and Spain,
    1952–1956   97
16 Exports of Oranges and Tangerines Expressed as a Per-
    centage of Output, Italy and Spain, 1952–1956   97
17 Prewar Output and Exports of Somali Bananas   100
18 Estimated Expenditures Under the Seven Year Develop-
    ment Plan   127
19 Estimated and Actual Expenditures for 1954 Under the
    Original Development Plan   128
20 Cumulative Totals of Annual Expenditures in 1954–1957,
    As Percentages of Estimated Total Expenditures Re-
    quired for Completion of the Revised Development Plan   129
21 Sources of Finance for the Development Plan   130
22 Public and Private Investment in Somalia, 1954–1957   132
23 Losses Incurred by the Somali Credit Institute, 1954–
    1957   142
24 Government Expenditures and Revenues in Somalia   147
25 The Balance of Payments of Somalia   150
26 Somalia's Exports Expressed As a Percentage of Imports,
    1895–1950   151
27 The Composition of Imports and Exports   153
28 Balance of Payments on Current Account by Monetary
    Areas   160
29 Imports by Monetary Areas   161
30 Repurchase of Somalos by CCMS   163
31 The Supply of Money in Somalia   163
32 Composition of the Note Cover   164

THE
ECONOMICS OF
TRUSTEESHIP
IN SOMALIA

[CHAPTER I]

Introduction

——— ❦ ———

POLITICS AND ECONOMICS IN AFRICA

THE CHIEF AIM OF THIS BOOK is to analyze the economic problems which an African country faces as it moves from a position of political and legal dependence toward the assumption of responsibilities for self-government in the modern world. In keeping with the current fashion, one may think of treating these problems as mere aspects or consequences of "underdevelopment." Such a treatment, however, does not go far enough. According to the prevailing (and perhaps not too satisfactory) definition, underdevelopment simply means poverty. There can be no doubt that African countries are poor. Some of them— such as Somalia, which is the country discussed in this book— are, as a matter of fact, abysmally poor. The need for development in Africa is great, but the sense of urgency that seems to exist about it cannot be explained by the mere fact of poverty.

The explanation, it is contended here, is to be found in a particular way of thinking about the relation of politics to economics.

The analytical categories of social science, such as those implied by the terms "politics" and "economics," have no exact counterpart in the real world. They exist only in the human fancy. The peculiar nature of the division of labor in social science is accounted for, in the main, by the complexity and indivisibility of the social process. Because the human mind cannot immediately master a complex subject in all its aspects, the task must be simplified by dividing the subject into smaller and more manageable parts, which can then be examined one at a time. But since the social process cannot actually be resolved into components, analysis can take place only in the human imagination. Certain commonly used phrases, such as, for example, "political and economic phenomena," may suggest to the unwary that the analytical categories of social science correspond to empirical realities. This, however, is a sheer illusion fostered by speech habits. That political and economic phenomena have no separate existence is clearly shown by the impossibility of determining the boundaries between them.

The proposition that the social process is indivisible is so widely accepted that it seems unnecessary to present additional supporting arguments. That men explicitly recognize the truth of a proposition does not mean, however, that their actions will always take it into account. This brings us to the heart of the issues to be discussed in this book; for in Africa today major policy decisions are frequently made on the implicit assumption that politics and economics represent independent spheres of social life.

Africa is the last continent in which European nations still possess sizable colonial empires. It is common knowledge, however, that the tide of anticolonialism which has swept Asia since the Second World War has also reached Africa. Some African territories have already achieved political independence, others are about to do so, and it may be only a matter of time before all of them acquire some form of self-government. Anticolonialism is, without doubt, one of the most important ideological forces of our time, and in the light of this fact it is hardly surprising to find an increasing number of Africans demanding that their dependent status be ended as soon as practicable. What is significant in this respect is that African nationalists tend to view the achievement of self-government as a task involving nothing more than changes in government personnel and machinery, and in law. The possibility that a modern nation-state, if it is to maintain itself with at least a tolerable degree of stability, may also require other changes in social organization is hardly ever given serious consideration. The possibility that changes in economic structure may also be needed is sometimes raised but is usually treated with suspicion, if not with outright hostility. The suggestion that economic difficulties may exist is apt to be regarded not as something to be examined in an objective spirit but as a political argument designed to frustrate what are felt to be the legitimate aspirations of colonial peoples. There is a feeling, in other words, that if the principle is accepted that the creation of modern nation-states depends upon the fulfillment of certain economic conditions, support will be given to the idea of maintaining colonial rule for a long time, perhaps even indefinitely. In part this feeling is engendered by the fact that the colonial powers have in postwar years engaged in large expenditures for the economic development of their African dependencies and that this policy is being interpreted in many quarters as a kind of *quid pro quo*, whereby Africans are to be offered economic assistance in exchange for the surrender, or at least the indefinite postponement, of their claims to political freedom. Whatever the reasons, the fact remains that the question of self-government

3

is almost invariably approached from a purely political stand-point and the economic aspects of the question are, as a consequence, dismissed as irrelevant. Such an approach logically presupposes the independent functioning of political and economic phenomena.

As soon, however, as a colonial power accedes to African demands for self-government, whether this be through an agreement for the immediate transfer of political power or through a definite commitment to allow the transfer to take place in the near future, a remarkable change of attitude takes place. African political leaders begin to place more emphasis on economic problems, to which they attach increasing importance as time goes on; eventually they become engaged in an anxious, sometimes even frantic, quest for a solution.

A common explanation of this change of attitude is that attainment of political independence causes the masses in underdeveloped countries to become acutely aware of the extent of their poverty and to long more intensely for a higher standard of living; for the masses, it is said, look upon political independence as something which will, among other things, open the door for new and quicker ways of satisfying their material aspirations. There is of course an element of truth in this view, but it must be pointed out that in any African country one can always find a number of people whose material aspirations have been rising for a long time, as well as a large segment of population for whom acceptance of existing conditions is still, despite the achievement of political independence, the prevailing outlook on life.

Actually, the chief reason behind the new concern with economics is political.[1] One of the effects which assumption of responsibility for the conduct of governmental affairs has on

[1] On this point see also W. Brand, *The Struggle for a Higher Standard of Living*, Glencoe, Illinois, 1958, pp. 7–8.

African political leaders is to bring them face to face with the melancholy fact that while economic forces cannot block the formal establishment of new states they can, on the other hand, impair the capacity of these states to function independently. But, as many people may well be tempted to ask, why should this be the case? Neither history nor logic supports the proposition that the creation of new states always and of necessity provokes adverse economic reactions. One of the major purposes of this book is to show that the answer to this highly important question is to be found in the economic structures of African countries. A detailed analysis of these structures and a careful study of their implications is therefore essential to an understanding of the problem. At this point it can only be noted that the economic structures of African countries result from processes which took many decades to evolve, during which time they were adapted to and conditioned by the then existing colonial régimes. Looking back, it seems regrettable that this should have occurred; yet it must be kept in mind that such things as investment patterns, trade channels, financial mechanisms, and the like, could not have been developed in a political and institutional vacuum. In any event it is fairly apparent that structural changes are now badly needed, since the existing structures are in several respects incompatible with the new political conditions. Unfortunately economic structures, because of inherent rigidities, cannot be changed with the same speed and ease as formal political institutions, and the result is a fundamental maladjustment between economic and political conditions which can threaten the stability and in some instances the very existence of the newly-born nation-states.

In what, then, might be called the "post-independence phase," African political leaders are quick to realize the need for economic development, that is, changes in the economic structures of their countries. What they are not prepared to accept is the fact that such changes take a long time. Such changes, they fear, may come too late to prevent serious damage to the young and fragile political institutions which many of them have helped to build and which they are understandably anxious to preserve. The time factor is thus seen as the major problem; indeed it may be said, to paraphrase one of S. H. Frankel's expressions, that in the eyes of African political leaders time appears to be the enemy, not the ally, of man.[2] Hence the insistence of these leaders that a way must be found of accelerating the process of economic development.

The solution to their problem, they believe, lies in economic planning. The reasons for this belief deserve close scrutiny. As is well known, planning is the subject of an old and still unresolved controversy among economists. Originally the controversy centered—and to a large extent still does—upon a question of economic equality. Advocates of economic planning contended that if a central plan were used instead of the market mechanism to co-ordinate economic activities, it would be possible to achieve equality of income and wealth without incurring losses in productivity and living standards. Their opponents, while conceding that the market economy necessarily involved inequalities, doubted that a planned economy could match the gains in living standards which are possible under the market system. Whether economic equality can be achieved through planning without incurring losses in productivity and living standards is an important and intellectually stimulating issue, but it is not one with which African political leaders are primarily and immediately concerned. Clearly, they are interested in rapid development, not economic equality; should it be shown that rapid development could be had at the cost of great differences in income and wealth, there is little reason to doubt that they would take the view that the cost was worth paying.

[2] *The Economic Impact on Underdeveloped Societies,* Cambridge, Massachusetts, 1953, p. 145.

One reason for the belief that planning will permit rapid development is the experience of Soviet Russia. Critical minds may wonder whether Soviet experience really justifies such a conclusion. They may argue, for instance, that the development of industrial power in Russia has not been accompanied by visible gains in the population's standard of living. They may also point out that it is not yet clear to what extent the development of Soviet industrial power is due to central planning and to what extent it is due to other factors, and that, as a consequence, it is far from certain that Soviet planning techniques can be successfully transferred to other parts of the world, such as Africa. But all this is actually beside the point. The fact is that African leaders, rightly or wrongly, do regard Soviet experience as proof that economic development can be accelerated through planning. But while they are ready to borrow economic techniques from Russia, they are on the other hand loath to adopt Russia's form of government. By and large Africans seem to prefer democracy, though some of them are evidently willing to embrace authoritarianism. Totalitarianism, however, they all reject, either because they feel it is undesirable, or because they think it is impractical under present conditions in Africa, or for both reasons. This selective approach to Russia's experience needs to be underscored, since again it shows how African thinking about public affairs is governed by the assumption that politics and economics represent independent spheres of social life. In practice it is of course impossible to divorce economic planning from totalitarian controls, and the result is that what goes under the name of economic planning in Africa has, apart from the term, little if anything in common with economic planning in Russia.

But Soviet experience, or, to put it more exactly, what Soviet experience allegedly shows in the way of possibilities of accelerating economic development, is not the only reason for the insistence on planning in Africa. Another is the belief that methods used in the political sphere can also be used with

7

success in the economic sphere. For the essence of planning is the attempt to solve economic problems by the methods of politics.

To make this point clear, we must briefly consider certain differences in the meaning of the term "politics" as that term is used by political scientists and economists. As used by political scientists, who are primarily interested in studying human conflicts, the term "politics" refers, in a general way, to the conduct of governmental affairs. As used by economists, it has a more specialized meaning; it refers to the fact that certain events are controlled solely by the human will. This, it will be recognized, is perhaps the most vital aspect of politics, since the conflicts which political scientists study are basically clashes between the wills of different human beings. The reason that this aspect of politics interests economists lies in one of its logical consequences: that events which are controlled entirely by the human will cannot be determined, even approximately, by reference to rational criteria. Where wages are set by collective bargaining, to cite a familiar example, the outcome cannot be known until the last moment in the negotiations between union and management. Supply and demand conditions determine the upper and lower limits for wages, but within these limits wages may be set anywhere. What they will ultimately be will depend upon whether union or management has been better able to make its will prevail. As this example shows, political forces may operate even where the state is not directly involved. Nevertheless the notion of politics is usually associated by both political scientists and economists with that of the state, since the state is, after all, the most powerful expression of the human will.

Though economics differs from politics, it must not be thought of as representing a set of objective forces. Indeed, scientific determination of the relation between politics and economics would be a relatively simple matter if, in contrast to the thoroughly subjective character of politics, economics could be described as purely objective. Unfortunately this is not the case. Economic forces contain subjective as well as objective elements, and the close intermingling of these often makes it hard to distinguish between them. It is precisely because of this difficulty that there is often a strong temptation for policy-makers to ignore the objective aspects of economic problems; for when these problems are viewed in an exclusively subjective light it no longer seems necessary to submit passively to certain rules or principles, and their solution can be conceived in political terms, that is, as depending solely upon human volition.

It is in this sense that planning can be described as an effort to solve economic problems by political means. The insistence that economic development must be planned is also closely related to and in part explained by a phenomenon which is a concomitant feature of the anticolonialist movement. This is the tendency to treat all social issues as if their political aspects (in the political scientist's sense of the term) were always and necessarily of overriding importance. It has already been seen, for example, how African recognition of the need for development is essentially brought about by political considerations (again, in the political scientist's sense of the term). But the primary reason for the confident view that planning will solve Africa's economic problems is the deep-seated belief, by no means limited to Africans, that there are no economic obstacles which the human will, provided that it be sufficiently strong and determined, cannot overcome, no matter how unfavorable the circumstances may be. It would indeed be difficult otherwise to understand how the United Nations Mission which visited East Africa in 1951 could state that in Somalia "developmental resources are scarce; hence planning is all the more important." [3]

Thus African anticolonialism, which at first seeks to achieve self-government in total disregard of economic factors and later

[3] U.N. Doc. T/1033, p. 20.

looks to planning for a solution of the economic problems that inevitably arise, is based on two implicit assumptions. One is that politics and economics represent independent spheres of human activity and the other that political methods can be effectively used to solve problems not only in the political but also in the economic sphere. Both of them reflect an unwillingness to recognize that the stability of self-governing states depends to some extent upon impersonal economic forces.

It may be that, in some measure at least, these observations apply to anticolonialism in general. If their scope is limited to Africa in this book it is because the transition from colonial to independent status on that continent involves important considerations which have little or no bearing on similar developments in other parts of the world. A substantial difference between Africa and Asia, for example, is that the latter, before it gained its new independence, already had a long tradition of statehood, that is, of political organization into large units based on impersonal relationships. The transition to modern nationhood in Asia did not therefore involve as drastic a change as it does in Africa, which lacks a similar tradition. In precolonial times most African territories knew only such forms of political organization as are essentially suited to small tribes and kinship groups.[4]

Another consideration is the state of scientific knowledge about African societies, a subject to which anthropological research has made, up to now, by far the largest contribution. It is only natural that anthropologists should wish to give the greatest possible weight, as they have done, to those aspects of human behavior in which they happen to be especially interested; but their disproportionate influence in this area of studies has served, in a subtle and indirect fashion, to reinforce an

[4] For an interesting historical study of this subject see D. Westermann, *Geschichte Afrikas,* Cologne, 1952.

already strong tendency in the minds of the non-African public and of policy-makers to minimize the role of economic forces in Africa. It is to be hoped that the rising interest which the outside world is currently showing in African efforts to join the family of nations on a footing of equality will spur on specialists in other branches of social science to play a greater part in the study of African affairs, and that as a result a more balanced approach to this subject may be eventually achieved. With more research and analysis by economists in particular, it will perhaps also be more readily appreciated how vital a role the price mechanism actually plays in regulating life in African societies.

THE EXPERIMENT IN SOMALIA

THERE IS perhaps no better way to illustrate the prevailing conception of the relation between politics and economics and its policy implications in Africa than to examine the consequences for Somalia of the United Nations decision to give that country its independence after a ten-year period of trusteeship beginning in 1950. In a sense, the decision meant that Somalia was to be the scene of an experiment in the feasibility of a new method of state-creation. Not that the United Nations, in making the decision, deliberately set out to carry out such an experiment, for there is no evidence to suggest that this was its intention; but the new method was to be tried in a country where conditions appeared to be so unfavorable that, if it really proved effective, one would be led to expect its use to meet with success almost anywhere else.

Before World War II, Somalia was an Italian colony.[5] Italian

[5] For the sake of brevity and in accordance with what appears to be growing usage, the Italian term "Somalia" will be used throughout the book to refer to the trust territory of Somaliland under Italian administration. The choice of the term was dictated by the fact that it would have been misleading to continue to refer to the territory as Italian Somaliland, as

influence in that area dates back to the end of the nineteenth century, though an effective system of colonial government was not introduced there until 1905. Previously, Somalia had been under the suzerainty of the Sultan of Zanzibar; the Sultan's authority, however, had been little more than nominal, and real political power had rested with the individual tribes and clans in the territory. As a political entity, therefore, Somalia came into being only when it fell under Italian control.

From the very beginning, its administration as a single political unit presented economic difficulties. There were large deficits in the colonial government's budget and in the balance of payments. The reason for them soon became evident: Somalia simply lacked the means to support a central administration. In subsequent years various attempts were made to improve the country's economy, principally through the development of banana, cotton, and sugar plantations. As a result Somalia became closely linked with and increasingly dependent upon the outside world, especially Italy. But the budget and the balance of payments continued to show deficits, which Italy had to meet through annual subsidies.

To Italy, therefore, Somalia was an economic liability. The justification for holding on to the territory was primarily strategic, inasmuch as Italy had long nourished the ambition of conquering Ethiopia. To this end it had acquired control of neighboring Eritrea, and Somalia, located as it was in the northeastern corner of Africa, represented another convenient place for massing troops and military equipment to carry out a swift invasion of Ethiopia whenever an opportunity would present itself. The invasion was finally ordered in 1935 by the Fascist régime then

was done before World War II, since the territory is no longer an Italian possession. At the same time, a way had to be found to prevent the trust territory from being confused with French Somaliland or the British Protectorate of Somaliland.

in power, and Italian soldiers poured across the border into Ethiopia from both Eritrea and Somalia.

But the Italian occupation of Ethiopia was a short-lived affair, as Italy lost all its African possessions during the Second World War. The former ruler of Ethiopia, Emperor Haile Selassie, regained his throne, and Britain's armies occupied Italy's other colonies—Libya, Eritrea, and Somalia. When, after the cessation of hostilities, the Big Four (the United States, Great Britain, France, and the Soviet Union) met to discuss the terms of a peace treaty with Italy, the question came up as to what to do with Italy's African colonies, excluding of course Ethiopia, which had in the meantime been restored to the status it had enjoyed before the Fascist invasion. The Big Four agreed that the colonies should not be returned to Italy; beyond this, however, they could not agree. As a way out of the impasse, they decided in 1947 to go ahead with the treaty just as it was and let the United Nations settle the thorny colonial question. This the United Nations did, albeit after numerous and lengthy debates.

Concerning Libya and Eritrea, it resolved that the former should become an independent kingdom and the latter should be federated with Ethiopia. But with regard to Somalia it reached a truly extraordinary decision. In 1949 it passed a resolution calling for the transformation of the territory into a sovereign state after a ten-year period of trusteeship under Italian administration. Italy subsequently signed a trusteeship agreement which conformed with the terms of the United Nations resolution. The agreement became effective on December 2, 1950, and Somalia thus became scheduled to acquire its independence ten years from that date. (Later, the deadline was advanced to July 1, 1960.) This meant that a sovereign state was to be created by a method for which there appears to be no historical precedent and which it would not be inappropriate to call the "deadline method."

This is not the place to give a detailed account of the United Nations debates on the disposition of the former Italian colonies, particularly since there already exists an abundant literature on the subject.[6] It is necessary, however, to discuss briefly the main considerations involved in the decision to put Somalia under Italian trusteeship for ten years.

There was, on the one hand, Italy's interest in the case. Italy was not a member of the United Nations then, but its position was eloquently presented and supported by the Latin American states. To be sure, Somalia no longer had any strategic advantages to offer, inasmuch as it was unthinkable that Italy should, in the light of past experience and of the prevailing climate of international opinion, plan another colonial venture into Ethiopia. As for economic benefits, Italy well knew that Somalia had none to offer (nor did, for that matter, any of its other former colonies). There were, however, certain prestige considerations which the democratic government that had come to power in the immediate postwar period felt it could not ignore. At the time the Big Four were discussing the terms of the peace treaty, it had plainly voiced its expectation that they would not treat Italy harshly, since Italy had, if only at the last moment, overthrown the Fascist régime and swung to the Allied side during the war. As a matter of fact, the peace treaty which Italy had to sign in 1947 was rather mild on the whole. In it, however, Italy was asked to renounce all its former colonies. At the same time an intense propaganda campaign was being waged in various quarters seeking to portray Italy as a nation particularly brutal in its treatment of colonial peoples. The situation invited a parallel with the case of Germany, which at the end of the First World War had been

[6] See, for example, D. A. Wainhouse and P. A. Mangano, "The Problem of the Former Italian Colonies at the Fourth Session of the General Assembly," *Department of State Bulletin*, XXII (1950); B. Rivlin, *The United Nations and the Italian Colonies*, New York, 1950; and G. H. Becker, Jr., *The Disposition of the Italian Colonies*, Annemasse, 1952.

forced to give up its colonies amidst a similar propaganda campaign. Italy naturally resented the implication that it was less
fit to administer colonies than other nations. While it did not
condone Fascist acts of aggression, the postwar government maintained that neither it nor the pre-Fascist democratic régimes
should be associated in the public mind with Fascist colonial
policy. By inducing the United Nations to give it at least a voice
in the administration of dependent territories, it hoped to win
international recognition of the legitimacy of its point of view.

On the other hand, there were the Afro-Asian states. Ideo-
logically they were committed to press for a grant of immediate
independence to colonial territories, or, if this were not possible,
for an unambiguous guarantee of independence in the near
future. Above all they were determined to avoid any line of
approach which would condition the grant of independence upon
the fulfillment of certain criteria, lest the final outcome be left
in doubt. Under the circumstances, one can understand why the
Afro-Asian states insisted that an Advisory Council—consisting
of representatives from Colombia, Egypt, and the Philippines—
be formed to act as a kind of United Nations "watchdog" in
Somalia under the trusteeship. One can also understand why the
trusteeship's duration was fixed at ten years. For it would be
wrong to imagine that in the choice of this period there entered
any element of rational calculation as to how long it would
actually take to prepare Somalia for independence. Ten years
was simply the longest period the Afro-Asian states could be
persuaded to accept as giving them no cause to suspect that in
agreeing to trusteeship for Somalia they were perhaps agreeing
to a form of disguised colonial annexation.

In devising the resolution which the United Nations adopted
in 1949, therefore, the guiding consideration was to find a politically acceptable compromise plan. Little attention was given
to the difficulties that might arise in the way of implementation,

despite some warnings. A few delegates expressed their qualms about the economic situation in Somalia. Moreover, the United Nations had in its hands the report of an investigating commission which the Big Four had sent to the former Italian colonies.[7] The report likewise stressed the existence of unfavorable economic conditions in Somalia. None of these warnings was taken seriously.

It was only after the trusteeship régime had gone into operation that the United Nations began to show concern over the economic problems that faced Somalia and threatened to rob the promise of independence by 1960 of much of its substance. In addition to the missions that visited East African trust territories (Somalia, Tanganyika, and Ruanda-Urundi) every three years as a matter of routine, the United Nations sent a special technical assistance team to Somalia to find out how the country's economic difficulties might be overcome. To this end it also urged the World Bank to send a mission, and the World Bank, albeit reluctantly, agreed to do it. None of the reports which the United Nations received, however, held out much hope for a solution. The United Nations, furthermore, urged the Italian Trusteeship Administration to formulate and carry out a development plan, and the Italian administration did its best to oblige. Notwithstanding all these efforts, it became apparent within a few years that the experiment in Somalia would have to be adjudged a failure, and a vast majority of the delegates at the United Nations, including those of the Afro-Asian states, reluctantly came to the conclusion that all that could be expected within the time limit set by the trusteeship agreement would be "nominal" independence, while the task of achieving "real" independence would have to be put off to the indefinite future.

[7] Four-Power Commission of Investigation for the Former Italian Colonies, *Report on Somaliland*, II, London, 1948.

ORGANIZATION OF THE BOOK

THE CHAPTERS that follow in this book are devoted to an analysis of the economy of the trust territory of Somalia, in order to demonstrate how economic forces can interfere with the attainment of political objectives and why attempts to cope with such forces by purely political methods are likely to prove futile. The analysis is thus intended as a case study of the general nature of the problems which certain preconceptions about the relation between politics and economics, as previously outlined, pose for Africa. As the reader will easily perceive by now, the situation in Somalia is admirably suited for such a study, in view of the special circumstances under which the trusteeship régime was set up.

Chapter II explains why, in view of the present state of statistical knowledge, an analysis of Somalia's economy must in the main be qualitative rather than quantitative. The next four chapters are devoted to an examination of the country's economic structure. Of these, the first three deal with individual sectors, while the last one takes up the basic features of the economy as a whole. This is then followed by a review of efforts to plan the country's economic development; there it is pointed out that such efforts did not succeed in, and probably were not aimed at, bringing about structural change. In Chapter VIII it is shown how, largely as a consequence of structural features, Somalia is unable without external subsidies to meet the costs of modern central government. In the last chapter the main conclusions are drawn and the need for a different approach to the relation between politics and economics is stressed. A note is also appended in which some of the possible implications that the recent establishment of the European Common Market may have for Somalia are briefly discussed.

Since this book is addressed primarily to the American reader, foreign units of measurement have been converted, wherever possible, into expressions more familiar to him. Monetary values, for instance, are quoted in dollars instead of liras or somalos; distances are given in miles instead of kilometers; land measurements are expressed in acres instead of hectares; and so on.

As a final item it may be mentioned that none of the chapters that follow contains a great deal of descriptive material. Factual information has been limited to the extent necessary to make clear certain points. To give less was not possible; and to give more would have tended to obscure the strictly analytical character of this study.

CHAPTER II

The Problem of Somali Statistics

THE MODERN trend in economic analysis calls for a quantitative approach when inquiring into the economic problems of an underdeveloped country. The importance of quantitative analysis lies not only in the interest it holds for scholars, but also in the fact that it constitutes an essential prerequisite to the formulation of a comprehensive development program. Owing to the lack of adequate statistics, however, it is not possible to apply this type of analysis to the economy of Somalia, since this would require the use of statistical parameters to analyze changes in income, productivity, standard of living, and other economic phenomena.

The need for more adequate statistics in Somalia is frequently emphasized at the United Nations.[1] To a large extent this preoccupation with statistics reflects a desire to accelerate the pace

---

[1] See, for example, U.N. Doc. A/3170, pp. 88–89 and 105.

of development in economically backward countries and an acceptance of the belief, widely held nowadays, that such a result can be achieved through comprehensive planning. Whether this belief is well founded is debatable, since the task of planning involves many difficult problems, both theoretical and practical. It would be premature, however, to consider these in reference to Somalia, since the statistical problem must be solved first. United Nations sources are therefore right in stressing the importance of statistics, but what their statements often imply about the nature of the solution of the statistical problem raises a highly significant question concerning the relation between politics and economics that is often overlooked.

For what is implied is that the solution depends solely upon a political decision rather than upon a change in economic and social conditions. To put matters more simply, it is suggested that statistical improvements depend entirely upon the willingness of governments to authorize the necessary expenditures for the provision of additional services. The report of the United Nations Technical Assistance mission which visited Somalia in 1951, for example, describes the statistical problem in these terms:

> Owing to the recent establishment of the Italian Administration, there are gaps in the technical and statistical materials—indeed very little in the way of basic economic statistics and research which are to be taken into consideration. Much work remains to be done along fundamental lines in the way of statistical organization, economic study and research before the Territory's problems can be fully understood.[2]

It then goes on to say:

> The United Nations provides technical assistance in these fields, but improvements in statistical organization and eco-

[2] U.N. Doc. ST/TAA/J/Somaliland/R.1, p. 3.

nomic study are essentially a responsibility of the Administering Authority.[3]

The report thus excludes the possibility that statistical difficulties may be due to impersonal factors, since it would make no sense otherwise to speak of the Administering Authority's, or any one else's, "responsibility."

As will be shown in a somewhat detailed examination of the present situation regarding basic statistics, statistical improvements in Somalia, contrary to what is implied in the statement quoted above, depend primarily upon changes in economic structure. What should be understood by basic statistics in this context are data on population, resources, national income, public revenues and expenditures, and international payments. These are "basic" in the sense that they form an indispensable minimum for development planning. How much additional information is available may determine, in part, the degree of adequacy of the plan, but without basic statistics there can be no planning at all.

POPULATION

THE BEST statistical information on Somalia's population is limited to the years 1931, 1950, and 1953. Only during those years did the Italian authorities make serious efforts to draw up a comprehensive picture of the country's demographic conditions.[4] Data on the size of the population for those particular years are summarized in Table 1.

As may be seen from the table, non-Somalis form a numerically insignificant proportion of the total population. It should be noted, however, that the term "Somalis" as used in the table is

[3] *Ibid.*, p. 3n.
[4] Partial and semiofficial estimates are available for several years before 1931, as well as for some years between 1931 and 1950, but are not included here because of their fragmentary character.

TABLE 1

POPULATION OF SOMALIA

GROUPS	1931	1950	1953
Somalis	1,019,904	1,242,199	1,263,584
Italians	1,631	4,107	4,916
Aliens	37	46	124
Total non-Somalis	1,668	4,153	5,040
Total population	**1,021,572**	**1,246,352**	**1,268,624**
Non-Somali population as % of total population	*0.2*	*0.4*	*0.4*

Source: Annual Reports of the Italian Government to the United Nations on Somalia.

somewhat misleading, since it includes other, though small, ethnic groups. Italian statisticians use the awkward term "autochthones" to designate this large segment of the population, but this is also inaccurate, since Asian immigrants are included. While it is difficult to find a precise word, it does not seem altogether improper to speak of "Somalis" in this case, since it is expected that the population classified by Italian statisticians as "autochthones" will correspond more or less to that of "Somali nationals" after 1960.[5] The ethnic distribution of the population is shown in Table 2. The data given there are for 1931 only, since no comparable statistics are available for 1950 and 1953, but it seems safe to assume that the ethnic distribution of the population has not varied significantly since 1931.

The last category in Table 2 consists for the most part of Asians—Arabs, Indians, and Pakistanis. Available statistics on the Asian population are summarized in Table 3, but it must be

[5] On the question of citizenship and national status in Somalia under the trusteeship, see the Annual Report of the Italian Government to the United Nations on Somalia, 1954, pp. 15–16. See also G. A. Costanzo, *Problèmes de la Coexistence de Groupements Ethniques Différents dans le Territoire de la Somalie sous Tutelle Italienne,* Document de Travail pour la 30e Session d'Etudes de l'Institut International des Civilisations Différentes, 1957, Doc. 26.

TABLE 2

ETHNIC DISTRIBUTION OF THE POPULATION,
EXCLUDING ITALIANS AND ALIENS

ETHNIC GROUPS	PER CENT OF TOTAL POPULATION
Somalis	90.5
Negroid groups	6.2
Others	3.3

Source: Istituto Centrale di Statistica. *VII Censimento
Generale della Popolazione*, V, Rome, 1935.

added that the figures cited there are only rough approximations.
The actual size of the Arab population is probably smaller than
indicated, since some of the people included in that group are
not Arabs, but Arabized Somalis. Arab influence has been present

TABLE 3

ASIAN POPULATION OF SOMALIA

ETHNIC GROUPS	1931	1950	1953
Arabs	18,000	23,000	30,000
Indians and Pakistanis	700	1,000	1,000
Total Asians	18,700	24,000	31,000

Sources: Istituto Centrale di Statistica, *VII Censimento Generale
della Popolazione*, V, Rome, 1935; Annual Reports of the Italian Government to the United Nations on Somalia.

for a long time in Somalia. Some historians have traced it as far
back as the seventh century A.D. Immigration from neighboring
Arabia, though apparently on a small scale, has been frequent
since then, and intermarriage between Somalis and Arabs, at
least since the eighteenth century, fairly common.[6] It is therefore difficult, if not impossible, to distinguish clearly between
Arab communities long established in Somalia and recent immi-

[6] See I. M. Lewis, *Peoples of the Horn of Africa*, London, 1955, p. 45;
E. Brotto, "Le Popolazioni della Somalia," *L'Italia in Africa*, ed. Comitato
per la Documentazione dell'Opera dell'Italia in Africa, Rome, 1955, I, pp.
179–80.

grants, and between Arabs and Arabized Somalis. This may explain why Italian census-takers have refrained from drawing a sharp line between Africans and Asians.

Of greater relevance to economic analysis than the ethnic composition is the occupational distribution of the population (Table 4). Despite an increase in the relative share of agriculture and a

TABLE 4

PERCENTAGE DISTRIBUTION OF THE SOMALI POPULATION
ACCORDING TO OCCUPATION

OCCUPATION	1931		1953	
Pastoralism	49.4	} 81.2	42.9	} 71.0
Pastoralism-agriculture	31.8		28.1	
Agriculture	7.9		19.0	
Trade	1.1		3.2	
Manual crafts	0.7		1.0	
Fishing and other maritime occupations	0.4		1.0	
Other	8.7		4.8	

Sources: Istituto Centrale di Statistica, *VII Censimento Generale della Popolazione*, V, Rome, 1935; Annual Reports of the Italian Government to the United Nations on Somalia.

decline in the relative share of pastoralism, it is evident that pastoralism, whether carried on in pure form or combined to some extent with agriculture, is still the principal Somali occupation. For reasons that will be discussed in the next chapter, herding in that part of the world is to a large extent associated with nomadism or seminomadism. Official statistics showing the extent of nomadism and seminomadism in Somalia are summarized in Table 5. It should be noted, however, that figures on the total sedentary population for 1950 and 1953 include occupants of mobile dwellings in Somali villages. It is possible that some or all of these people are actually nomads or seminomads who took up temporary residence in villages at the time the estimates were made. If so, their number should be subtracted from that of the total sedentary population and added to that of nomadic and seminomadic groups (figures in parentheses, Table 5). Either way, there is a close correspondence between the number of nomads and seminomads on the one hand and the combined total of pastoralists and pastoralists-agriculturists on the other, as may be observed by comparing the figures in Tables 4 and 5.

TABLE 5

PERCENTAGE DISTRIBUTION OF THE SOMALI POPULATION
ACCORDING TO MODE OF LIVING

GROUPS	1931	1950	1953
Nomadic and seminomadic	82.6	69.6 (75.5?)	67.5 (75.5?)
Sedentary	17.4	30.4 (24.5?)	32.5 (24.5?)

Sources: Istituto Centrale di Statistica, *VII Censimento Generale della Popolazione*, V, Rome, 1935; Annual Reports of the Italian Government to the United Nations on Somalia.

The only remaining item of any interest is that of population density. The available information shows Somalia to be a country of sparse and unevenly distributed population. The greatest concentration is found in central Somalia, that is, in the area between the Uebi Scebeli and the Juba, the only two rivers of any importance in that country. Population density is lowest in the Migiurtinia and Mudugh regions, which comprise, roughly speaking, the area northeast of the Uebi Scebeli. In the westernmost portion of the country, that is, in the area across the Juba, density is only slightly higher than in northeastern Somalia. A summary of statistics on population density for 1953 is given in Table 6.

This completes the statistical picture of Somalia's population. For purposes of economic analysis and programming, it is extremely unsatisfactory. In the first place, there are large gaps in the picture. No data, for example, have been gathered on the distribution of the population according to sex and age

TABLE 6

POPULATION DENSITY OF SOMALIA, EXCLUDING ITALIANS
AND ALIENS, 1953

AREA	SQUARE MILES	POPULATION	POPULATION PER SQUARE MILE
Migiurtinia and Mudugh	80,881	223,773	3
Interfluvial zone	55,409	880,897	16
Trans-Juba	41,911	158,914	4
Total Somalia	178,201	1,263,584	7

Source: Annual Report of the Italian Government to the United Nations on Somalia, 1954.

groups, apart from an Italian expert's preliminary inquiries which, in any event, have been limited to urban centers.[7] Secondly, the statistics that are available are subject to wide margins of error. This point deserves some elaboration, since insufficient awareness of the high degree of unreliability of Somali population statistics can easily lead to faulty interpretations and conclusions.

For example, the terms chosen for designating different statistical sources are apt to result in some confusion. Somali population figures for 1950 and 1953 were calculated by the Italian Administration in Somalia (*Amministrazione Fiduciaria Italiana della Somalia,* commonly known as AFIS) and officially labeled as "estimates." On the other hand, data for 1931 were compiled by the Italian Central Institute of Statistics and officially described as the result of a "census." This difference in terminology has apparently encouraged some people to impute a fairly high degree of reliability to the 1931 figures. The United Nations report previously cited, for instance, speaks of the 1931 census as a "rather exhaustive" count, which "provided for the first time a fairly complete account of the population."[8] Unfortunately this view is largely incorrect. The 1931 figures were offi-

[7] See Annual Report of the Italian Government to the United Nations on Somalia, 1955, pp. 149–50.
[8] U.N. Doc. ST/TAA/J/Somaliland/R.1, p. 39.

26

cially described as the result of a "census" because a calculation of Somalia's population was made in that year as part of a general census covering Italy and all Italian dependencies overseas. Standard census procedures, however, were applied only to non-Somalis and to approximately nine per cent of the Somali population. The remainder was estimated on the basis of information supplied by tribal chiefs and notables. The Italian census report itself expressed grave doubts about the reliability of the estimate.[9] There is therefore no reason for believing that the 1931 figures were any more precise than the AFIS estimates of later years. AFIS made its calculations independently of censuses in metropolitan Italy and this fact explains its more modest but also more accurate terminology.

It is sometimes asserted, on the basis of a comparison of statistical data for different years, that there is a definite trend toward population increase in Somalia.[10] The validity of this statement, however, depends on the margin of error that can be properly attributed to the statistics in question. In its annual report to the United Nations on the administration of Somalia, the Italian Ministry of Foreign Affairs states that, in the opinion of AFIS, the margin of error for the 1950 and 1953 population figures is about 10 per cent (plus or minus). This statement is accompanied by the observation that it is practically impossible to make an exact calculation of the margin of error.[11] In other words, the AFIS estimate is based to some extent on guesswork, and it does not exclude the possibility that the margin of error may actually be larger than indicated. Table 7 shows some of the different annual rates of population change that are possible for the period 1931–1953, if we take the margin of error to be 10 per cent (plus or minus). Although no calculation of the

[9] Istituto Centrale di Statistica, *VII Censimento Generale della Popolazione*, V, Rome, 1935, pp. *4–*9.

[10] U.N. Doc. ST/TAA/J/Somaliland/R.1, p. 39; Lewis, *op. cit.*, pp. 48–49.

[11] Report for 1950, p. 161, and for 1953, p. 343.

margin of error for 1931 has ever been published, it seems reasonable to assume, in view of what has already been said about the method of enumeration used in that year, that the margin was at least as large as that of more recent population estimates.

TABLE 7

POSSIBLE ANNUAL RATES OF CHANGE OF THE SOMALI POPULATION FOR 1931–1953, ON THE ASSUMPTION OF A MARGIN OF ERROR OF ±10%

ADJUSTMENT IN 1931 DATA (%)	ADJUSTMENT IN 1953 DATA (%)	ANNUAL RATE OF CHANGE
0	0	+1.1
+10	0	+0.5
0	+10	+1.6
−10	+10	+2.3
+10	−10	0.0

Thus we see in Table 7 that if we assume no error in the statistical data for both years, we obtain an annual rate of population increase of 1.1 per cent. If we decrease the 1931 figure by 10 per cent and increase the 1953 figure by the same percentage, we obtain a much higher rate of increase (2.3 per cent). But if we increase the 1931 figure by 10 per cent and adjust the 1953 figure by the same margin in the opposite direction, the annual rate falls to zero. If we were to assume a larger margin of error—say 15 per cent, which is by no means unrealistic—it might even be possible to show a decline in population. Any statement to the effect that the Somali population is increasing is therefore open to doubt. The only assertion that seems reasonable in this case is that there is no evidence of any radical change in the size of the Somali population.

There can therefore be no doubt that Somali population statistics, although they provide us with a certain amount of information, are of limited value. Probably the most useful purpose they can serve is to indicate, in a rough and approximate way, the orders of magnitude involved.

In view of this situation, it is not surprising to hear so many voices in the United Nations urging that something be done to obtain more precise population statistics. Whether anything can be done, however, depends on the possibility of removing the barriers which have prevented the taking of an adequate census thus far.

The first obstacle that must be considered is the high opportunity costs that inevitably would occur in Somalia's government budget if a true census were organized. The Italian Trusteeship Administration has pointed out time and again that any effort to improve population statistics would entail large expenditures, since additional means and personnel would be required. Such expenditures would be reflected in the Somali budget in the form of opportunity costs regardless of the source and method of financing used to meet them. For if no additional sources of revenue, domestic or foreign, were to be found, the new expenditures could be met only by reducing commitments to other categories in the budget; if a new source of revenue were found, a cost would still be incurred in the form of opportunities foregone to use the funds thus raised for other purposes, as, for example, for health or education.

If it were solely a matter of opportunity costs, however, the barrier to better statistics would not be insuperable. Whether the sacrifice involved is worth making or not is an important issue, but one which, in the final account, can be resolved only on the basis of value-judgment. Unfortunately the problem is not so simple, for there are other factors to consider.

As previously indicated, more than two-thirds of the population consists of nomads and seminomads. Somalia is a vast country (about 178,000 square miles), most of it is scrubland, and the existing network of roads and other modern means of communication is poor. Even if financial difficulties could be overcome, there would still be the technical question as to whether it is possible to make a precise calculation of a largely nomadic population in so unfavorable an environment. Experts who have been studying this question have not come up with a solution so far, and there is apparently not much hope that any will ever be found.[12]

Nor is this all. Success in the collection of statistics, particularly of census information, requires a certain measure of cooperation by the population which is made the object of inquiry, but the Somalis apparently are not yet ready to co-operate in the required degree. Somali unco-operativeness was one of the major factors cited by the Central Institute of Statistics for its inability to provide adequate census data in 1931, and there is no reason to believe that there has been any substantial change in Somali behavior since then. As reported by the Institute, Somali unco-operativeness was largely due to fears of increased taxation.[13] Although taxation was not the purpose of the Institute's inquiries, Somali fears were not altogether unfounded. For it must be admitted that, regardless of the purpose for which they may be intended, the results of statistical investigations are always useful to the authorities for increasing the efficiency of tax collections. Consequently, if the Somalis are to become more co-operative in regard to census-taking, their attitudes concerning taxation will also have to change. Taxation is an unpopular subject everywhere, but in Somalia, as in probably all underdeveloped countries, there is an extreme reluctance to pay taxes. In part this is explained by the wretched poverty of the majority of the people, but another important factor is the low level of general education. Most Somalis, according to two United Na-

[12] See the statement by the special representative of the Administering Authority to the Trusteeship Council, U.N. Doc. A/3170, p. 89.

[13] VII Censimento, V, p. *9.

tions missions which looked closely into this matter, do not seem to understand that tax revenues are badly needed to pay for essential public services.[14] Thus poverty and lack of education combine to produce a deep-rooted aversion to the payment of taxes, and this attitude in turn produces suspicion and uncooperativeness in regard to any kind of statistical investigation.

RESOURCES

STATISTICS ON Somalia's resources suffer from the same weaknesses as those on population. The information available is too limited and consists to a large extent of vague and unreliable estimates. Though such information is not altogether useless, since it permits us to express the orders of magnitude involved, it is inadequate to be considered an inventory of the country's resources.

The factors which account for the inadequate statistics on population play an equally important role in the case of resources. To these factors, however, we must add the dual character of the economy, that is, the division of the economy into a market sector and a subsistence sector. The latter is quite large, including, according to a recent estimate, as many as 90 per cent of the population.[15]

The principal resources are livestock and various agricultural crops. The general impression conveyed by the statistics available is that the number of livestock is quite substantial. Estimates vary, however, and in some cases vary considerably, as shown in Table 8. Estimates of the suitability of land for pastoral and agricultural purposes also show the importance of livestock. Grazing land forms about 43 per cent of the total surface, while the land suitable for cultivation amounts to only 18 per cent

[14] U.N. Doc. T/1033, p. 27; U.N. Doc. T/1200, p. 18.
[15] U.N. Doc. A/3170, pp. 98–99.

TABLE 8

Estimates of Livestock Population

(*Thousands of Heads*)

Source and date	Cattle	Camels	Goats	Sheep
UN, 1950	1,200	1,200	2,100	2,000
AFIS, 1952	800	1,300	2,900	600
IBRD, 1956	1,200	1,100	2,000	800

(Table 9). It is interesting to note, however, that only a small proportion of the cultivable land is actually used. In 1957 this proportion was about 10 per cent (about two million acres) and in previous years it was even smaller. If only land is considered, therefore, even after allowing for substantial errors in the estimates, there is ample room for agricultural expansion, although the Somali economy appears destined to remain predominantly pastoral.

TABLE 9

Land Distribution According to Potential Use

Land Classification	Millions of Acres
Grazing	49.4
Cultivable	19.8
Uncultivable	44.7

Source: Annual Report of the Italian Government to the United Nations on Somalia, 1957.

The principal crops raised in Somalia are durra, corn, sesame, bananas, cotton, and sugar cane. Of these, the first three are raised primarily for direct consumption, while the remainder form part of the market economy. Estimates of land devoted to these crops and of output in recent years are summarized in Table 10.

These estimates, it is worth repeating, are only rough approximations, and their usefulness is further impaired by the absence of statistical measurement in value terms. The failure to provide an expression of values constitutes, without doubt, the

TABLE 10

AREA AND PRODUCTION OF PRINCIPAL CROPS

	1952		1953		1954		1955	
CROP	Thous. of Acres	Hun. of Tons	Thous. of Acres	Hun. of Tons	Thous. of Acres	Hun. of Tons	Thous. of Acres	Hun. of Tons
Durra	150	500	70	100	700	1,000	1,200	600
Corn	60	300	30	100	60	200	200	600
Sesame	40	20	20	15	20	20	30	50
Bananas	10	400	15	700	20	600	20	800
Cotton	60	25	20	2	20	3	30	10
Sugar cane	5	600	5	800	5	1,000	5	1,300

Sources: Annual Reports of the Italian Government to the United Nations on Somalia; U.N. Doc. T/1296. Figures have been rounded.

biggest gap in the statistical picture of Somalia's resources, since measurement based on physical units alone cannot serve the ends of economic calculation and comparison.

To illustrate this point, let us consider the question of the relative importance of Somali livestock and agricultural resources. It is generally believed that livestock outranks agriculture in importance. This is, of course, true in some sense. It is true, as we have seen, in the sense that the majority of the population is engaged in raising livestock, as well as in the sense that more land is available for grazing than for cultivation. Between physical magnitudes and values, however, there is no necessary connection. The value of certain resources exploited by a minority of the population may exceed that of resources exploited by the majority. It is also possible for a small area of land to yield greater values than a large one. No conclusion concerning the relative value of resources can therefore be drawn from statistical expressions of physical magnitudes. To determine such value, it is necessary to have a record of money prices. Unfortunately, most of Somalia's livestock and many crops do not enter the market but are used for direct consumption instead, and a record of the money prices of the few resources that do enter the market would obviously not suffice in this case. So long, therefore, as so many of the country's resources remain outside the market economy, their relative value cannot be known.

NATIONAL AND PER CAPITA INCOME

THE FACTORS which have prevented the compilation of a reliable census of population and resources have also discouraged official efforts to draw up a record of national income accounts. All that we have on this subject are rough estimates by the Italian economist Malagodi. The results of his calculations, which are limited to the year 1952, are summarized in Table 11.

TABLE 11
NATIONAL AND PER CAPITA INCOME OF SOMALIA

INCOME	U.S. $ EQUIVALENTS
National	28,000,000
Per capita	
Market sector	134
Subsistence sector	13
Somalia as a whole	22

Source: G. F. Malagodi, *Linee Programmatiche per lo Sviluppo Economico e Sociale della Somalia*, Rome, 1953.

In justice to Malagodi, it must be pointed out that he was fully aware of the difficulties inherent in the task when he attempted these calculations. He admitted that a large element of guesswork entered into them, particularly into those concerning valuation of the subsistence sector's output. Nevertheless he believed that his figures could be used safely if a margin of error of 15 per cent (plus or minus) were allowed for. The national income figure of 28 million dollars should therefore be taken to mean that, in Malagodi's opinion, the national income of Somalia lies somewhere between 24 and 32 million dollars. Moreover, it should be noted that per capita income figures in this case are not intended to provide a comparative index of the population's standard of living. As such they would obviously be too low. An annual income per head of 13 dollars, which is the figure cited for the subsistence sector, is so low as not to permit even physical survival. In the intent of the author, per capita income figures must be understood as expressions of orders of magnitude designed to show the weakness of the Somali economy, particularly of the subsistence sector, and the consequent high degree of dependence on foreign economic assistance. Even so, one may doubt the usefulness of the figures, since the same conclusions can be brought out more effectively through an analysis of public finance and balance of payments data.

PUBLIC FINANCE AND INTERNATIONAL PAYMENTS

FOR THE years following the establishment of trusteeship, public finance and balance of payments statistics present no special problems of reliability and adequacy. If one were to extend the time series so as to include data for periods prior to 1950, that is, those of British occupation and Italian colonial administration, it would be difficult to make meaningful comparisons in view of the numerous changes—as in size of territory, in type and value of currency, and in policy orientation—which occurred during that long period. For an analysis of current problems of public finance and international payments, however, the data available for the trusteeship period appear to be satisfactory. They are not presented here, but a detailed examination of them will be found in Chapter VIII.

From the standpoint of reliability and adequacy, therefore, statistics on the public budget and the balance of payments offer a sharp contrast to those on population, resources, and national income. On reflection, it is easy to account for the difference. For in the case of public finance and international payments the relative cost of statistical services is low, and the other and more fundamental obstacles to census-taking and social accounting can exert no influence. A realization of this difference and of the reasons for it can only add weight to the previous argument that it is necessary to recognize the nature of the obstacles if one is to avoid building false hopes about the possibility of obtaining data suitable for quantitative analysis and the mapping of an overall economic program.

STATISTICS AND ECONOMIC DEVELOPMENT

To SUMMARIZE, then, the problem of Somali statistics arises out of the inadequacy of the existing data for a quantitative analysis of the type essential to the blueprinting of a comprehensive development program. For such an analysis it is necessary to have detailed information on at least the following topics: population, resources, national income, public revenues and expenditures, and international payments. Only on the two last-mentioned items are the available statistics adequate, while on the remaining ones they are for the most part unreliable as well as insufficient. Among the factors responsible for these deficiencies the most important are: (1) high opportunity costs of additional statistical facilities; (2) nomadism and related environmental factors; (3) popular distrust of statistical inquiries, primarily out of fear of taxation, which in turn is largely due to low incomes and lack of education; and (4) the dual character of the economy.

These factors must be eliminated, or at least their influence must be sharply reduced, if there is to be any significant improvement in the collection and organization of Somali statistics. In principle this is not an unattainable goal, but one that will require a substantial measure of economic development. We are thus led to a seemingly paradoxical conclusion, since, on the one hand, statistics are viewed as an essential condition for the programming of economic development, while on the other hand it is evident that they can become available only as a result of economic development.

The paradox is more apparent than real, however, and is due to neglect of an important time element. For economic development is not a single event, but a long and multiphased process. What the statistical difficulties encountered in Somalia actually seem to suggest, when viewed in relation to economic development, is that in the initial phase of the process an underdeveloped country has no choice but to forego the advantages that programming might have to offer. If development does take place, this will entail changes in economic structure which eventually will reach a point where the collection of basic statistical information will no longer pose serious problems. For successful development will inevitably cause the subsistence sector to shrink to minor proportions, lessen resistance to taxation (through higher incomes and the spread of education), reduce the opportunity costs of statistical services, and so on. At that point the country will be ready to enter a new phase of the development process, in which programming, to facilitate the achievement of a further rise in the material standard of living, may be usefully considered.

Somalia must still be regarded as being in that initial stage of development. A quantitative analysis of Somalia's economy is clearly not feasible and must be replaced with a qualitative analysis. The latter is still important, for, while it cannot serve as a basis for programming, it can nevertheless provide broad guides for policy. This of course does not mean that all statistics must be shunned; whenever they are found to be adequate, they can still help to illuminate particular issues. In the main, however, the analysis must be qualitative, and to this type of analysis we shall now turn.

[CHAPTER III]

The Pastoral Economy

Somalia is an extremely poor country. In the popular view this fact is explained as the result of insufficient natural resources. This view, however, implies a basic misconception, in that it exaggerates the role that natural resources play in the determination of income disparities among nations. Natural resources are but one factor of production, one element in a complex network of mutually determining forces.

It is possible to arrive at a better explanation of Somalia's poverty through an analysis of the country's economic structure, a task that will occupy us in this and in the three chapters that follow. For an analysis of this type it is convenient to conceive of the Somali economy as divided into three sectors: the pastoral sector (or economy), indigenous agriculture, and the plantation sector (or economy). The first and the last of these terms are reasonably clear and require no definition, but a word may be said about indigenous agriculture.

The Pastoral Economy

In the literature dealing with Africa it is common to speak of "traditional" rather than "indigenous" agriculture. The term "traditional agriculture" is apparently derived from anthropological usage; it suggests, however vaguely, that African economic activities are governed by customary or irrational forces, in contrast to European or Western activities, which are presumably organized in accordance with rational principles. Such notions are questionable, and it seems more reasonable to assume that economic activities everywhere are governed by a mixture of rational and irrational motives. Indigenous agriculture, as used here, simply means subsistence agriculture. The latter term would be more acceptable because of its greater accuracy, but the possibility of its being confused with the subsistence sector of a dual economy has counseled against its use. For indigenous agriculture is only a part of the subsistence sector, herding being also a subsistence activity. In other words, the Somali economy has a dual character, and pastoralism and indigenous agriculture represent mere subdivisions of the subsistence sector; if they are treated separately here, it is because there are important differences between them which might otherwise become blurred.

It is perhaps hardly necessary to add that the division of the Somali economy into three sectors is merely an analytical device designed to facilitate understanding of the country's economic structure. Minor subsistence activities, such as hunting or fishing, are omitted from the discussion, inasmuch as they have little or no influence on the basic structural characteristics of the country's economy, and their inclusion would consequently only add unnecessary complications. For the same reason no mention is made of various small activities within the market economy, most of which are in one way or another related to production on the plantations. In this simplified treatment, therefore, the plantation sector and the market economy of Somalia are to be regarded as one and the same.

39

This chapter deals with the Somali pastoral economy, the central features of which are (a) a low level of commercialization and (b) livestock accumulation. The task of analysis in this case is twofold: in the first place it is necessary to explain why, in view of the abundance of livestock, so few animals and animal products are marketed; and secondly, it is necessary to explain why Somali herders persist, despite the low level of commercialization, in trying to enlarge their already sizable herds. It should become clear in the course of the analysis that these two questions are actually parts of a single problem, since the low level of commercialization and the accumulation of livestock are mutually related phenomena; the same set of basic factors that accounts for the one also accounts for the other. Before attempting an explanation of these phenomena, however, it seems appropriate to clear up certain facts concerning the level of commercialization.

THE LOW LEVEL OF COMMERCIALIZATION

IN CONSIDERING the level of commercialization of livestock resources, it is important to distinguish between external and internal markets. For reasons already discussed in the preceding chapter, statistical evidence can be used to support the assertion that the level is low only in so far as this refers to export trade. Nevertheless there is little ground for doubting the widely held belief that domestic markets absorb but a small proportion of the balance of supply (that is, after exports). Two observable facts may be cited which tend to support this conclusion. One is the marked reluctance of the Somali herder to sell livestock, or to put it more precisely, his unwillingness in most circumstances to part with any animals except those which, either because they are too old or for some other reason, offer no further breeding possibilities. As a result fewer livestock products, especially meat and hides, enter the market than the size of existing herds would seem to justify.[1] The other fact worth citing is the weakness of demand for the pastoral economy's products in the other domestic sectors. Indigenous agriculture is the second largest sector in terms of population, but its productivity is low and as a consequence it can command, on the average, only a small quantity of goods in exchange from other sectors. Purchasing power, for the sector as a whole as well as on a per capita basis, is higher in the plantation economy; there, however, it is the small size of the population that limits the sector's capacity to absorb livestock and livestock products. Thus neither indigenous agriculture nor the plantation sector, though for opposite reasons, can, under existing circumstances, provide a substantial outlet for the products of the pastoral economy.

As for the role of livestock and livestock products in external markets, the availability of foreign trade statistics makes it possible to determine the share of these products in the country's total exports. In principle, if a commodity's share of the value of total exports is small, it does not automatically follow that the level of commercialization of that commodity is low, inasmuch as the level of commercialization refers to the relation between the supply of a good and that part of the supply which enters the market, and it is by no means inconceivable that the proportion that is marketed may be high at a time when the good in question plays a relatively minor role in foreign trade. Of course, if it were statistically possible to determine this proportion for Somali livestock resources, it would be unnecessary to consider their importance in foreign trade and the ensuing complications, but the scarcity and unreliability of existing data concerning supply preclude such a direct approach. Taking into account, however, (1) that animal husbandry is the principal occupation of the majority of the Somali population, (2) that continual

[1] U.N. Doc. ST/TAA/J/Somaliland/R.1, p. 62; U.N. Doc. T/1200, p. 32; A. Maugini, "Lineamenti dell'Economia Rurale della Somalia," *Rivista di Agricoltura Subtropicale e Tropicale*, XLVII (1953), p. 219.

41

and often successful efforts are made to increase the size of herds, and (3) that domestic markets offer a narrowly limited outlet for animal products, it seems safe to conclude that a small share in the value of total exports reflects, among other things, a low level of commercialization.

Whether the share is actually small, and if so to what extent, can be ascertained by recourse to a simple statistical device, which consists of expressing the value of certain exported commodities —in this case livestock and livestock products—as a percentage of the value of total exports. Certain qualifications are necessary, however, for if used indiscriminately this device can be extremely misleading.

In the first place, although the ratio of the value of animal exports to that of total exports provides a useful measure of the pastoral economy's contribution to Somalia's export trade, it is not the only measure that ought to be considered. Relative and absolute values may move unequally or in opposite directions, and it would be dangerous in such cases to rely on relative values alone. In 1946, for instance, animal products represented about 60 per cent of the value of total exports, while in the following year the ratio stood at about 54 per cent. During this period, therefore, the ratio declined by 10 per cent; on the other hand the absolute value of animal exports rose by approximately 40 per cent. Thereafter their value, expressed as a percentage of total exports, continued to drop sharply; whereas in absolute terms it continued to rise for a while, then started to taper off, as can be seen from the following table showing animal exports for 1946–1951.[2] Only in 1952 did a new trend set in, as the value of

[2] U.N. Doc. ST/TAA/J/Somaliland/R.1, pp. 64 and 81. This report contains data on the value of animal exports expressed as a percentage of total exports and on the value of total exports. In reading the report the difference in trends shown by relative and absolute values is not immediately apparent, because the two sets of statistics are published in different sections and in connection with different issues.

42

YEAR	ABSOLUTE VALUES		RELATIVE VALUES	
	Thousands of U.S. $ equiv.	*Percentage change*	*Per cent of total exports*	*Percentage change*
1946	1,077		60.5	
1947	1,515	+40	54.3	−10
1948	1,560	+ 3	49.6	− 9
1949	1,419	− 9	43.2	−13
1950	1,372	− 3	38.8	−10
1951	1,347	− 2	32.1	−17

animal products began to move slightly upward, both relatively and absolutely.[3]

Secondly, it would be unwise to include the statistical data of periods in which the pattern of production and trade is temporarily disrupted by a major political crisis. Under normal conditions the pattern of production and trade changes only in response to the dictates of economic policy and the interplay of market forces. Because the same pattern is not likely to prevail in a period of political crisis, it seems best to leave the data for such a period out of account, except, of course, in those cases where the crisis leads to lasting changes. Thus in the decade that immediately preceded the Second World War, the general pattern of Somalia's export trade was, except for the short period of the Italo-Ethiopian conflict, basically the same as that which has obtained since 1952. Then as now, bananas formed by far the greatest proportion of exports, while animal products played a relatively minor role. In 1938, for example, bananas represented about 42 per cent of the value of total exports, while livestock and livestock products amounted to a mere 7 per cent. In 1952, the shares of bananas and animal products were 59 and 9 per cent, respectively.[4] The direction of trade was also essentially the same.

[3] See Table 12, this chapter.
[4] In rounded figures. For 1938 see M. Casilli d'Aragona, "Note sulla Economia Attuale della Somalia Italiana," *Rassegna Economica dell'Africa Italiana*, XXVII (1939), pp. 952–83, and G. Rocchetti, "Gli Scambi Com-

Then as now, bananas were shipped exclusively to Italy, while livestock and livestock products went for the most part to Aden, Kenya, Zanzibar, and other sterling-zone markets.[5] With the outbreak of the Second World War and the British military occupation that followed, the pattern changed, owing to the closing of the Italian market to Somali products throughout most of this period. As a result the banana industry came to a virtual standstill, whereas animal exports, intended for sterling-zone markets, continued more or less at the same level as before.[6] The high percentage figures in this period, therefore, do not indicate a sudden rise in the importance of animal exports. What they do indicate is a temporary but drastic contraction of total exports, as a result of the virtual disappearance of bananas.[7] Following the establishment of the trusteeship régime in 1950, the old pattern of production and trade reasserted itself.[8] It took some time, however, to reorganize production on the banana plantations, and it was not until 1952 that export trade statistics began to give evidence of the return to a normal pattern of trade.

Thirdly, if the period is so chosen as to involve the use of more than one domestic currency in the expression of export data,

merciali della Somalia," *Rivista di Agricoltura Subtropicale e Tropicale,* XLIX (1955), p. 282. For 1952 see U.N. Doc. T/1296, p. 123, and Table 12, this chapter.

[5] Casilli d'Aragona; U.N. Doc. T/1200, pp. 23–24.

[6] U.N. Doc. ST/TAA/J/Somaliland/R.1, p. 83; G. Rocchetti, "La Banani-coltura della Somalia," *Rivista di Agricoltura Subtropicale e Tropicale,* L (1956), pp. 87–89.

[7] But cf. U.N. Doc. ST/TAA/J/Somaliland/R.1, p. 63.

[8] An exception to this is the case of salt, which before the war was exported exclusively to Japan. The latter eventually turned to other sources of supply, and in consequence salt exports from Somalia ceased altogether. Salt, however, was never a significant export item. In 1938, for instance, it represented only about 4 per cent of the value of total exports. See Rocchetti, "Gli Scambi Commerciali della Somalia," p. 262. For a fuller discussion of this question see A. Festa, "Saline dell'A.O.I.," *Materie Prime d'Italia e dell'Impero,* III (1938); G. Lusini, "Le Saline Somale," *Affrica,* III (1948); M. Colombo, "Il Sale di Ras Hafun," *Affrica,* V (1950).

difficult exchange rate problems are bound to arise. It is a note-worthy fact that during the last thirty years no fewer than three different currencies have been used as domestic money in Somalia. Before the Second World War, when Somalia was an Italian colony, Italian money was used; during the British occupation that followed, the East African shilling replaced the Italian lira; and with the advent of trusteeship in 1950 a new currency, the somalo, took the place of the shilling. Consequently, if a long period is chosen, possibly because one might wish to compare postwar with prewar data, it becomes essential to find a common denominator of values. At first it may seem as if this problem could be solved by expressing export values in terms of a single foreign currency, such as the United States dollar, for example, using whatever exchange rate prevailed in each given year as the basis of conversion; on more careful examination, however, it will be seen that the dollar figures thus obtained will tend to give a substantially distorted picture of total exports as well as of the animal products' share of that total. There are two reasons for this: one is frequent fluctuation of exchange rates and the other, radical changes in the exchange rate system.[9]

According to the theory of foreign exchanges, the exchange rate is part of a system of mutual determination involving all the forces behind the demand and supply of internationally traded goods and services. Clearly, a change in the exchange rate can have no bearing on goods and services which remain wholly outside the international market throughout the period considered. It follows that for periods of fluctuating exchange rates expressions in terms of foreign currency equivalents of the value of exclusively domestic trade are definitely unreliable; they are bound to show changes in the market value of goods when none occurred, or none when changes did occur.

[9] For some of the different exchange rates that prevailed after 1932, see U.N. Doc. ST/TAA/J/Somaliland/R.1, p. 81.

The relevance of these considerations to Somalia's export trade stems from certain characteristics of the latter. As previously noted, postwar Somali exports tend to follow the prewar pattern, in that bananas form the largest proportion of exports and are marketed exclusively in Italy. In prewar days, however, Italy and Somalia had a common currency, and so long as this was the case the banana trade was in a sense domestic rather than international in character. The same can be said of trade carried on exclusively between Somalia and British territories in which the East African shilling circulated as domestic currency during the interval of British occupation of Somalia. If applied to periods of fluctuating exchange rates, therefore, statistical expressions in dollars (or any other foreign currency) are apt to convey an erroneous picture of actual magnitudes and movements of Somalia's external trade.

The error is certain to be even larger if a change in the exchange rate system occurs. For several years before the war the Italian exchange rate was pegged by means of exchange control which the Italian Government imposed unilaterally; after the war the price of the East African shilling, and later of the somalo, was set by international agreement, that is, in accordance with the rules of the International Monetary Fund. Under these conditions exchange rates do not provide a suitable basis for comparing postwar and prewar exports from Somalia, since official exchange rates which reflect an overvaluation of domestic currency, as is invariably the case with foreign exchange control, cannot be compared with rates which, ordinarily, either are equal to or tend to approximate market values.

Fourthly, account must be taken of different methods which may be used in the valuation of exports. The importance of this is vividly illustrated by official trade statistics, which almost invariably understate the value of total exports from Somalia. These statistics are usually compiled from information provided by customs records, and the reason for the understatement is to be found in the methods of valuation used at the customs. In principle, all goods as they pass through Somali customs are valued on the basis of f.o.b. prices, but in practice many items are calculated on the basis of arbitrary formulas designed to simplify the work of customs officials. Although these formulas are revised from time to time, discrepancies inevitably arise between the f.o.b. prices as computed at the customs and those actually paid. For most goods the discrepancies are small and insignificant, but in the case of bananas a substantial undervaluation occurs.[10] As a consequence total exports, as shown in official trade statistics, are also undervalued, while animal exports, when expressed as a percentage of total exports, are overvalued.

Lastly, it should be noted that United Nations and World Bank statistics purporting to show the size of the pastoral economy's contribution to Somalia's export trade for various years give the values of all items classified as "animals and animal products" in official Italian documents. The Italian classification, however, refers to both domesticated and wild animals. Fortunately, the statistical error resulting from the inclusion of leopard skins, ivory, rhinoceros horns, and similar items, appears to be fairly small for recent years.[11]

The statistical data which are believed to show the relative importance of livestock and livestock products in the export trade of Somalia are presented in Table 12. The years chosen are 1952–1955. Data for 1956, though available, have been omitted because exports in that year were sharply affected by the Suez Canal crisis. The data presented are by and large the same as

[10] See Annual Report of the Italian Government to the United Nations on Somalia, 1953, p. 363; U.N. Doc. T/1200, p. 22; U.N. Doc. T/1296, p. 123.

[11] Cf. the statistics cited in U.N. Doc. ST/TAA/J/Somaliland/R.1, pp. 64 and 90, and in U.N. Doc. T/1296, p. 9, with those in Annual Report of the Italian Government to the United Nations on Somalia, 1956, pp. 186–89.

those which appear in the World Bank Mission's report on Somalia. The only difference of any consequence is that the values of hides and skins, as given in Table 12, refer to domesticated animals only.

TABLE 12

ROLE OF LIVESTOCK AND LIVESTOCK PRODUCTS
IN SOMALIA'S EXPORT TRADE

ITEM	1952			1953		
	A	B	C	A	B	C
Hides and skins	659	70.1	6.2	776	63.9	9.0
Clarified butter	203	21.6	2.0	283	23.3	3.3
Live animals	56	6.0	0.5	110	9.1	1.3
Animal fats	22	2.3	0.2	31	2.6	0.4
Meat products	—	—	—	13	1.1	0.1
Total	940	100.0	8.9	1,213	100.0	14.1

ITEM	1954			1955		
	A	B	C	A	B	C
Hides and skins	744	54.9	8.1	1,027	58.5	9.0
Clarified butter	439	32.4	4.8	407	23.2	3.6
Live animals	159	11.7	1.7	317	18.0	2.8
Animal fats	—	—	—	—	—	—
Meat products	13	1.0	0.1	5	0.3	0.0
Total	1,355	100.0	14.7	1,756	100.0	15.4

Sources: Annual Reports of the Italian Government to the United Nations on Somalia; U.N. Doc. T/1296. Column A shows value of exports in thousands of U.S. dollar equivalents. Column B expresses this value as a percentage of total exports of livestock and livestock products, while Column C expresses it as a percentage of all exports, valued at actual f.o.b. prices.

By examining the table it will be seen that the value of livestock and livestock products exported, expressed as a percentage of total exports, ranged in this period from 8.9 to 15.4. The average was 13.3. Hides and skins made up the bulk of animal exports, while live animals accounted for a negligible share. Thus both the volume and the composition of trade support the conclusion that the level of commercialization of Somali livestock resources is low externally as well as internally.

THE ACCUMULATION OF LIVESTOCK

WE NOW turn our attention to the problem of livestock accumulation. As we have seen, the commercialization of animal products, in view of its low level, cannot explain the presence of sizable herds and the persistent efforts of herders to enlarge them still further. The question arises, therefore, whether livestock has any other uses which may account for its accumulation.

A chief function of livestock is to provide the pastoralist with the direct means for subsistence. To the extent that the pastoralist markets animal products he does so largely out of a desire to supplement, whenever possible, the meager supplies of his household with those goods (tea, sugar, cereals, textiles, etc.) which he cannot obtain directly from his herds. Livestock, however, is the principal source of food for the pastoralist and his family. It supplies them with milk, the principal item in their diet, and with clarified butter. Livestock is also a source of meat, although meat does not play as important a role in the pastoralist's daily diet as dairy products.[12] Large numbers of animals are slaughtered during certain rituals and ceremonies, as on the occasion of marriage or during religious celebrations; otherwise the pastoralist tends to limit his consumption of meat to certain periods when, because of seasonal factors, his herds fail temporarily to supply him with dairy products.[13] In certain Trans-Juba districts there are herders who drink the blood of cattle. They use techniques—which, incidentally, are also found in

[12] This is clearly shown in a study of nutrition in Somalia by G. Ferro-Luzzi, an F.A.O. expert. A summary of Ferro-Luzzi's conclusions will be found in the Annual Report of the Italian Government to the United Nations on Somalia, 1953, p. 445.

[13] L. Bozzi and G. A. Triulzi, "Osservazioni sugli Animali Domestici Allevati in Somalia," *Rivista di Agricoltura Subtropicale e Tropicale*, XLVII (1953), p. 280; I. M. Lewis, *Peoples of the Horn of Africa*, London, 1955, p. 67, fn. 2.

many other parts of Africa—that make it possible to draw the blood from the animals without killing them.[14] Livestock is, moreover, a source of hides and skins, from which sandals, belts, and other items used by the Somali household are made. In addition, camels are generally used as pack animals.[15] In a few instances bulls are used for this purpose, and among certain herders who also practice farming, bulls are sometimes used for ploughing.[16]

In addition to subsistence, livestock has several social uses. In traditional Somali society, marriage requires payment of bride-wealth (the so-called "bride-price") to the father of the bride, and payment is customarily made with livestock. In case of moral or physical injury to persons, including homicide, or of damage to property, the customary law of the Somalis calls for payment of compensation for damages, and this payment is, likewise, traditionally fixed in terms of livestock.[17]

The social significance of livestock is accentuated by prestige considerations, since the Somalis look upon pastoralism as a superior way of life. The more closely is an individual's way of living associated with livestock the higher is his status, and pure pastoralists consider themselves to be of noble origin. In the days which preceded European occupation of the country, tilling the soil was a task often assigned to slaves; today, despite the abolition of slavery, many Somalis continue to regard agricultural occupations as degrading.

In the view of competent observers, despite the uncertainties which surround statistics on the number of animals available in the country, there can be no doubt that the total supply of livestock exceeds the requirements of the population at present con-

[14] Lewis, *op. cit.*, p. 67.

[15] It may be of some interest to note that in Somalia camels are rarely used for riding purposes.

[16] A. Cortinois, "Cotonicoltura e Mezzi di Trasporto nella Somalia Italiana," *Rivista Coloniale*, V (1908), p. 65; Lewis, *op. cit.*, p. 68.

[17] Lewis, *op. cit.*, pp. 106–38.

sumption levels.[18] Subsistence uses, therefore, cannot be relied upon to furnish an adequate explanation of the accumulation of livestock.

As for social uses, important as these may be, it must be noted that they do not belong in the same category as subsistence functions. The latter involve acts of consumption which decrease the size of the national capital, while the former imply nothing more than a transfer of assets within the economy. Although, generally speaking, internal transfers of assets in the form of money may alter the volume of consumption in relation to savings, particularly if they occur between groups with different marginal propensities to consume, the same considerations do not apply to transfers of livestock within a pastoral economy of the type which has been described. A change in aggregate consumption is not likely to follow such transfers, and if it should, it is not apt to be significant.[19]

It is sometimes said that the accumulation of livestock in excess of the requirements of direct subsistence and commercial exchange represents a form of investment.[20] It is difficult, however, to accept this view. For if a good is to be treated as capital, it should be shown that it is needed for purposes of production; in this case it is not apparent that the excess of livestock is de-

[18] W. E. Corfitzen and G. Kinzy, *Preliminary Report on Somalia Agricultural Projects,* USOM/Italy, 1950, p. 14; T. M. Bettini, "Problemi Zootecnici della Somalia," *Rivista di Agricoltura Subtropicale e Tropicale,* XLVII (1953), pp. 263–64.

[19] One reason that the effects of transfer are apt to be minimal is that in many instances payment of bride-wealth involves no loss of livestock to people outside the tribe or clan. Bettini reports ("Die Rinderzucht in Italienisch-Ostafrika," *Koloniale Völkerkunde I,* Wiener Beiträge zur Kulturgeschichte und Linguistik, VI, 1944, pp. 114–15) that among the Ogaden and several other Somali groups divorce is rare, single women often marry relatives, and widows are ordinarily expected to marry close relatives of their former husbands.

[20] M. P. Gorini, "L'Oltregiuba, Com'è e Come Potrà Essere," *Agricoltura Coloniale,* XX (1926), pp. 258–59; Corfitzen and Kinzy, *op. cit.,* pp. 13–14.

signed to serve productive ends. When economic resources are kept idle, they may be legitimately described as representing some kind of investment potential, but not as actual capital. It seems more plausible, therefore, to treat the accumulation of livestock as a form of hoarding, as G. Mainardi does,[21] but even this approach requires an explanation of the economic ends such hoarding is intended to serve.

THE THEORY OF THE CATTLE COMPLEX

THE ACCUMULATION of livestock is not a uniquely Somali phenomenon. It is found among pastoral peoples throughout eastern Africa. It is found among the Nuer of the Sudan, the Masai of Kenya, the Karamajong of Uganda, the Watussi of Ruanda-Urundi, the Tonga of Northern Rhodesia, to cite just a few names and places. To be sure there are individual differences. Different religions call for different ritual practices involving livestock. Environmental and other factors explain the presence or absence of certain animals, such as camels. But the phenomenon's principal features—limited commercialization, reluctance to sell animals with breeding capabilities, payment with livestock of bride-price and of compensation for damages, avoidance of slaughter of animals except for ceremonial purposes or in case of emergency, belief in the superiority of herding as a way of life—these are to be found throughout the eastern portion of the continent, south of Egypt.

Anthropologists, who have been studying Africa longer than other social scientists, have shown a keen interest in this widespread phenomenon. Having recognized that there is no simple and easy explanation for it, they have developed a provocative theory, of which there are several versions, but which generally

[21] "L'Economia Agricolo-Pastorale della Somalia," *VIII Congresso Internazionale di Agricoltura Tropicale e Subtropicale,* II, Rome, 1938, p. 452.

relies on social and psychological factors as the key elements in the solution of the problem.

The theory is known as the "cattle complex." [22] Its main ideas are summarized by one writer as follows:

> It has often been observed that among African herders the wealthy man who owns vast numbers of flocks can scarcely be said to put these to any economic use whatsoever. What he actually needs for his family and household, ample and plural though these may be, amounts but to a fraction of what he owns in flocks and might, if he chose, dispose of in return for something else. This, however, he refuses to do. Instead, he permits his flocks to multiply; in fact, he exerts persistent and not infrequently successful efforts in this direction—and lets it go at that. The number of animals in his flocks is to the African herder and breeder a source of joy and pride. His social prestige goes up with the size of his herds. The fact that his cattle or sheep or goats are fine specimens exalts his ego immensely. As a wealthy and successful herder, he is a great and admirable man, envied by those less fortunate. But this is where the matter ends. From our economic standpoint the whole business represents little but waste of energy and effort; but our standpoint is not that of the Africans. [23]

Here one can easily see what the central point of the theory is. Africans, it is maintained, do not value livestock in the same terms as Europeans or Americans do. To the latter, quality, in the sense of ability to produce large quantities of milk and meat, is the important factor. Should a European be confronted with a choice between a small and a large herd, he would be inclined to choose the former if he expected to obtain a larger quantity of

[22] It is not usual for anthropologists to refer to the cattle complex as a "theory." The approach used here, however, requires that a sharp line be drawn between facts and their explanation, since only the latter is considered in this book. The former are not in issue.

[23] A. Goldenweiser, *Anthropology*, New York, 1937, p. 153. Quoted by permission of the publishers, F. S. Croft and Co.

milk and meat from it. The African, on the other hand, is more interested in the number than in the quality of animals. What prompts him to amass vast herds with little or no regard for their productivity, it is said, is that he is able in this way to achieve high social standing in his community.[24] Thus the essence of the cattle-complex theory is that the accumulation of livestock in eastern Africa represents a case of "conspicuous waste."

Anthropologists, however, do not agree on all aspects of the cattle complex. Some of them attach considerable importance to the role of subsistence while others minimize it, although there is general agreement that subsistence is secondary to social uses and prestige considerations.[25] Moreover, there is no agreement on the definition of the cattle complex, and individual formulations are often couched in vague terms. One writer, for instance, defines the cattle complex as "a kind of identification with cattle which leads to their association with ritual (and presumably religion) as well as many other things." [26] Another, on the basis of investigations among the Jie of Uganda and the Turkana of Kenya, uses a sociological approach. He sees the phenomenon as "an institutional complex of 'stock association'" in which "a man is in the centre of a specific field of interpersonal relations based on ties of kinship and bond-friendship, and these relations are chiefly, though not wholly, expressed and maintained through a system of reciprocal rights in respect of domestic animals." [27] A third writer concludes from his intensive research among the Nuer of the Sudan that "irrespective of use" cattle are "in themselves a cultural end," only this time it is psychological elements

[24] On this point see also *Report of the Kenya Land Commission*, 1934 (Cmd. 4556), pp. 359–61, 497; T. R. Batten, *Problems of African Development*, London, 1954, Part I, pp. 63–64.

[25] H. K. Schneider, "The Subsistence Role of Cattle Among the Pakot and in East Africa," *American Anthropologist*, LIX (1957).

[26] Schneider, *ibid.*, p. 278.

[27] P. H. Gulliver, *The Family Herds*, London, 1955, p. 244.

which are stressed. "So many physical, psychological, and social requirements can be satisfied from this one source," he writes, "that Nuer attention instead of being diffused in a variety of directions, tends, with undue exclusiveness, to be focused on this single object and to be introvertive, since the object has a certain identity with themselves."[28] Thus individual formulations and approaches to the cattle complex differ in several respects, but regardless of differences one always finds that primary, if not exclusive, emphasis is put on irrational elements of human behavior as the key to the solution of the problem.[29]

It may be asked at this point why so much attention is paid to anthropological ideas in what is claimed to be an economic analysis. There are three important reasons for this.

One is the wide influence of the cattle-complex theory. Not only is the theory extensively discussed in anthropological literature, as might be expected, but references to it can also be found in the writings of economists.[30] Official reports on conditions in East African territories, such as Belgian reports to the United Nations on Ruanda-Urundi and British reports on Tanganyika, describe livestock problems in terms which show the unmistakable influence of the cattle-complex theory. The same can be said of some United Nations reports on Somalia. Thus the United

[28] E. E. Evans-Pritchard, *The Nuer*, London, 1940, pp. 40–41.

[29] The critical remarks made above as well as those that follow in the text should not be misunderstood. The writings of these anthropologists are being viewed here solely with reference to a particular issue of economic importance. Anthropologists are interested in many other things, and a large part of their efforts is usually devoted to detailed description of life among primitive or, as some of them prefer to say, "non-literate" peoples. Nothing that is said here, therefore, should be interpreted as aiming to cast doubt on the value of the contribution which the works cited in this chapter have made to the field of anthropology in general or on the high standards of scholarship so clearly displayed by their authors.

[30] See, for example, W. A. Lewis, *The Theory of Economic Growth*, Homewood, Illinois, 1955, pp. 26, 43, 227; P. T. Bauer and B. S. Yamey, *The Economics of Underdeveloped Countries*, London, 1957, pp. 28–29.

Nations visiting mission which went to Somalia in 1951 described Somali herders as interested in increasing the number rather than the quality of animals; it also emphasized the connection between this attitude and the payment of bride-price as well as prestige factors.[31]

Another reason is that the cattle-complex theory raises a serious issue concerning the claim of economic science to universality and independence. For its principal point is that livestock in eastern Africa, though a scarce resource no less than anywhere else, is not governed by economic considerations. If this is true, it follows that the analytical tools of economics cannot be used to explain any aspect of animal husbandry in eastern Africa. It is thus implied that economic science does not apply to all mankind, but depends for its validity and usefulness upon the existence of specific cultural and social institutions. In other words, economic studies should be subordinated to the so-called "behavioral sciences." These implications of the cattle-complex theory remind one of the views and criticisms voiced long ago by Veblen and other institutionalists, and before them by the adherents of the German Historical School of economics. Viewed against this background, it is indeed not surprising to find the Veblenian concept of "conspicuous waste" being given so prominent a role in the theory of the cattle complex.

Finally, the cattle-complex theory has significant implications for economic policy. If the theory is correct, there can obviously be little hope of mobilizing the resources of the pastoral economy for the general development of the country unless the herder can be persuaded to change his outlook on livestock. The logical task of government, in the light of this theory, is therefore one of propaganda and persuasion. As a matter of fact, the

[31] U.N. Doc. T/1033, p. 4. The mission that visited Somalia in 1954, on the other hand, appeared to have some doubts about this matter, judging from the noncommittal language of its report. See U.N. Doc. T/1200, pp. 32–33.

first United Nations visiting mission to go to Somalia did call for a policy aimed at imparting "a new set of social and economic values" to the Somali people.[32] But this raises an issue of practical importance. For if it should turn out that the theory is either incorrect or rests on false assumptions, a policy of persuasion might have disastrous consequences, as later discussion of the livestock problem will show.

The theory of the cattle complex that will be discussed here is the one expounded by Melville J. Herskovits, an eminent American anthropologist. It was Herskovits who coined the term "cattle complex," but more important than this is the fact that his treatment of the subject is broad and comprehensive, whereas other views are usually based on observations of a single tribe or area.

In fairness to Herskovits, it must be said at the outset that he expressly excludes the Somalis from the East African "cattle area," as he calls it, in which the characteristics of the cattle complex are to be found. The reason that he gives for excluding the Somalis is that they raise other animals in addition to cattle.[33] But Herskovits also speaks of a "prestige system," which is geographically a more inclusive concept, since according to his definition it covers, in addition to the peoples of the East African cattle area, some Sudanese tribes as well as those pastoral groups of the East African Horn which "lie outside the cultural dominance of the literate Amharic groups." [34] Thus the Somalis are included in the "prestige system," though they are not mentioned by name. According to Herskovits, the distinguishing feature of the cattle complex is the use of cattle for the payment

[32] U.N. Doc. T/1033, p. 24.
[33] "The Cattle Complex in East Africa," *American Anthropologist*, XXVIII (1926), pp. 648–49.
[34] "Peoples and Cultures of Sub-Saharan Africa," *The Annals of the American Academy of Political and Social Science*, CCXCVIII (March, 1955), p. 16.

of bride-price and as compensation for damages.[35] This feature, however, is also found in the more inclusive "prestige system." The only distinction, then, is that the "prestige system" in eastern Africa includes pastoral peoples who raise other animals in addition to cattle and use them as means of payment on the occasions which have been cited.

The distinction may have some special significance for anthropologists.[36] Where, however, the problem of livestock accumulation is viewed solely from an economic standpoint, it obviously makes little difference whether hoarding is limited to cattle or whether it also involves camels or sheep. Here, therefore, the distinction will be ignored.

The basic reason for the accumulation of livestock, according to Herskovits, is the desire for prestige. Cattle, he says, "are merely possessed and esteemed for the prestige their possession brings." [37] The desire for prestige is universal and is often attained through display of scarce goods. As Herskovits puts it: "For in the vast majority of cultures the position of those in power is established, continued, and constantly strengthened by the prestige that derives from elaborate display and consumption of economically valuable goods." [38]

Among the pastoral peoples of eastern Africa, this universal craving for prestige finds its expression in the accumulation and display of livestock. Economic considerations, if they enter into the picture at all, play a definitely secondary role.

Wealth, as defined in these societies, is restricted to the principal animal herded, and its acquisition is a man's primary ambition. Because wealth, and the prestige associated

---

[35] "The Cattle Complex in East Africa," pp. 361–88, 524–28.

[36] See P. H. Gulliver, "A Preliminary Survey of the Turkana," *Communications from the School of African Studies*, N.S., No. 26 (University of Cape Town, 1951), p. 16.

[37] *Economic Anthropology*, New York, 1952, p. 265.

[38] *Ibid.*, p. 462.

with it, is in these societies counted in terms of the number of beasts a man possesses, it is to his advantage to have the largest number of head possible. Considerations of quality, opportunities to exchange his animals for other goods, and the idea of consuming them as food have only recently begun to enter.[39]

As may be seen from the above quotation, the accumulation of livestock gives a man prestige because it represents wealth. But here a question arises as to the meaning of wealth in a situation where neither consumption nor commercial exchange is quantitatively important.

One possibility is that livestock may be used as money, in which case it may be said to represent command over wealth. This possibility is suggested by the fact that livestock is used as means of payment in acquiring a wife or in compensating someone for damages. Herskovits, however, is most emphatic in rejecting the view that livestock is money. He points out that except in the two instances cited livestock does not serve as a medium of exchange. Moreover, it fails to act as a "least common denominator of values." [40]

On this issue Herskovits is undoubtedly right. From an economic point of view the most significant function of money is that it promotes the efficiency of production by making it possible to compare costs. Despite the fact that some uses of livestock in eastern Africa suggest functions which might be described as "quasi-monetary," it is obvious that they do not serve, and are not intended to serve, the ends of economic calculation.

Having thus rejected the idea that livestock is money, Herskovits seeks to define wealth in terms that would fit his argument that livestock is accumulated primarily for the sake of prestige. This leads him to formulate a concept which he calls "economic surplus."

[39] "Peoples and Cultures," p. 17.
[40] *Economic Anthropology,* pp. 245, 265.

According to Herskovits, the total output of goods and services in any society can be classified under two headings: the requirements of subsistence and the excess over those requirements. Up to a point this classification resembles the popular distinction between necessities and luxuries. In the popular conception, however, the distinction lacks precision, thereby permitting its use in different contexts and making an immediate assessment of its general validity extremely difficult. Herskovits' classification, on the other hand, has a precise and unique meaning.

To avoid possible confusion, it should be noted that Herskovits' definition of subsistence differs from that which appears in Ricardian theory. As is well known, Ricardo assigns some role to the habits of the community in determining the level of subsistence (though it must be admitted that his concept of subsistence lacks clarity in certain respects), whereas Herskovits defines the requirements of subsistence as that bare minimum which is needed for physical survival.[41] Of course Herskovits does not deny that man is something more than an animal and that as man he has numerous other requirements. These, however, he calls "wants," which are culturally determined, and are to be distinguished from "needs," which are physiological in nature.[42]

The satisfaction of these "wants" is possible only if output exceeds the quantity required to meet physical "needs." This excess is the "economic surplus." It may be used in a variety of ways, but its ultimate function is to satisfy, directly or indirectly, the desire for prestige. Often, particularly in technologically primitive societies, this is achieved through sheer display of the economic surplus.[43]

[41] *Economic Anthropology*, pp. 395–96.
[42] *Ibid.*, pp. 5–6.
[43] *Ibid.*, pp. 395–415, 461–83.

This, then, is how Herskovits seeks to explain the accumulation of livestock in eastern Africa. Hoarding of livestock results in prestige for the owner because livestock represents wealth, in the sense of an excess over the requirements of physical survival.

CRITICISM OF THE THEORY

THE THEORY of the cattle complex has a certain amount of superficial plausibility. It is nevertheless untenable. To provide an adequate explanation of livestock accumulation in eastern Africa, the theory depends in a vital manner upon the concept of economic surplus. Without the latter, it cannot account for the prestige that is derived from hoarding the largest possible number of animals. This dependence upon the concept of economic surplus is the theory's greatest weakness. For the concept is woefully deficient, not in one but in several respects.

To begin with, let us consider the claim that the concept is applicable to all societies. The objection to this claim is that the problems of economic life are thus grossly oversimplified. A rich man may spend a fortune in order to be able to hang a genuine Rembrandt on a wall of his living room or only a few dollars on a mediocre painting by some obscure artist, but surely neither the difference in the value of the two paintings nor the motives which may induce the rich man to purchase one of them, or both, can be explained simply by reference to an economic surplus. As a general tool of analysis the concept of economic surplus is too crude to be of much use. This point seems so obvious as to need no belaboring.

Another and even more serious problem concerns the economic surplus concept's operational meaning. As formulated by Herskovits, the concept is clearly intended to serve as an objective criterion, since it implies measurability, at least in principle. While this makes it singularly attractive to the scientific mind, note must be taken of the fact that, as an objective criterion, the concept plays no practical role in the daily decisions which people everywhere have to make with regard to the allocation of economic resources. Indeed it cannot do so. For the material requirements of physical survival are determinable only by reference to nutritional and other medical standards, and it is obvious that ordinary people, especially those living under technologically primitive conditions, lack the knowledge that would enable them to decide where to draw the line between "subsistence" and "economic surplus." Nevertheless it is upon their decisions that the creation of such a surplus depends. Such decisions, if they are to take into account the difference between "needs" and "wants," can only be based upon individual conceptions of what is necessary for life. Conceptions of this kind are essentially subjective and are apt to coincide with the requirements of survival only in the rarest of cases. More often than not they will exceed these requirements by some margin.[44]

Use of the concept in connection with the hoarding of livestock in eastern Africa raises still another important question. If it is true that livestock is accumulated primarily to satisfy a desire for prestige, while economic considerations are largely ignored, and that this prestige is acquired through display of goods which represent wealth in the sense of an excess over the requirements of survival, why is it that surpluses of other goods are not utilized in the same manner? Among the Somalis, if a man accumulates agricultural products in excess of the requirements of survival or even of his own conception of what is essential for life, as he sometimes does, he is not likely to enjoy

[44] H. W. Pearson ("The Economy Has No Surplus," in *Trade and Market in the Early Empires*, ed. K. Polanyi *et al.*, Glencoe, Illinois, 1957) goes so far as to claim that it is impossible to measure the economic surplus and that the concept is therefore meaningless. But cf. M. Harris, "The Economy Has No Surplus?", *American Anthropologist*, LXI (1959).

much prestige because of it.[45] How is one, then, to explain the fact that prestige is associated with livestock but with no other good?

Herskovits' only answer is that such matters are determined by custom and convention.[46] By implication it is thus admitted that the concept of economic surplus is not sufficient to account for the hoarding of livestock and the prestige that is derived from this activity. Moreover, the statement that such activity is customary among pastoral peoples in eastern Africa is merely a statement of fact which the theory of the cattle complex is supposed to explain. A chain of reasoning which in the end leads back to the original problem as a conclusion is to a large extent circular.

As an analytical tool, therefore, the concept of economic surplus suffers from so many serious deficiencies as to be of little value. Once it is eliminated from the theory of the cattle complex, however, the latter breaks down. For without it, the theory cannot explain the accumulation of livestock in Somalia or in any other part of eastern Africa. These difficulties, it may be added, are largely the consequence of an unwarranted effort to substitute anthropological for economic concepts. They only go to show that where the phenomena to be explained involve allocation of scarce resources—be they in Western, African, or any other society—anthropology cannot, any more than any other social science, provide a substitute for economic analysis.

[45] For instance, it was known as far back as in the days before World War I that certain Somali groups, such as the Abgal, which possessed no livestock, were in the habit of hoarding sizable amounts of sesame. There is no indication, however, of any sense of prestige being associated with this activity in the manner and degree that is usually associated with livestock. See R. Onor, *La Somalia Italiana*, Turin, 1925, p. 69.

[46] *Cultural Anthropology*, New York, 1955, p. 164.

The Precautionary Motive in Hoarding Livestock

THE EXPLANATION of livestock hoarding that is presented here is based on certain specific assumptions that are applicable only to the situation in Somalia. Formulated in more abstract terms, the same explanation can be easily fitted to the more general case of livestock accumulation in eastern Africa. Since, however, the principal concern here is with the structure of Somalia's economy, considerations of relevance require that the discussion be confined to the livestock problem as it manifests itself in Somalia.

The first important factor that must be taken into account is the scarcity of water. There are only two rivers in Somalia, the Juba and the Uebi Scebeli, both of which rise in Ethiopia. Of the two the Juba is unquestionably the more important watercourse. Its average flow in normal years is three times that of the Uebi Scebeli. It is practically perennial, its lower channel having been known to run dry for one or two months only once every fifteen or twenty years, while the lower channel of the Uebi Scebeli is dry for about two months almost every year. Moreover the water of the Juba is always fresh, whereas that which flows in the lower course of the Uebi Scebeli is apt to be brackish between flood periods. Both rivers normally rise in flood from March to May and from October to December. In addition to these rivers, there are also a number of small streams; all of them, however, are intermittent. The total supply of surface water is therefore quite limited.

There is also ground water, and the Somalis have dug a large number of wells. Because of limited technological knowledge and the scarcity of capital, however, the Somalis must use relatively simple and labor-intensive methods which do not permit them to excavate wells beyond a certain depth. This means that only relatively shallow aquifers can be tapped, and the supply of ground water that can be obtained from them is, for several reasons, sharply limited. To begin with, rainfall is generally low and unevenly distributed, mean annual precipitation ranging from thirty-three inches in some areas to less than one inch in others. Though the Somalis distinguish two rainy seasons, one from April to June and another from September to November, precipitation is irregular, so that a short period of drenching rains followed by a long and severe drought is by no means uncommon. In addition to rainfall being low and irregular, there are a number of factors—such as high evaporation, rapid runoff owing to topographical conditions, and others—which make it difficult for precipitation to reach the ground-water table even where soils are sufficiently permeable. Humidity is high almost everywhere in Somalia, and in view of this fact it may seem strange that there should also be a high rate of evaporation. The explanation, however, is to be found in wind and temperature conditions. Somalia is almost continually swept by monsoons, and temperatures range from 60 degrees Fahrenheit to 110, the average for the country being about 90 degrees. Thus high temperatures and wind movements combine to produce rapid evaporation, notwithstanding the high humidity of the area. Because of rapid evaporation, along with the other factors mentioned, recharge and storage of ground water are apt to be low in many places. The quantity of available ground water is therefore limited, and the quantity of usable water is even smaller, since quality is extremely variable. In the coastal lowlands the ground-water table frequently lies only an inch, or even less, above mean sea level, and the result is salt-water contamination. Inland the ground water is often alkaline, owing to the presence of sodium, calcium sulfate, magnesium sulfate, and other chemical substances. The degree of mineralization of the underflow varies greatly. In some instances it makes the water unsuitable for

6 5

irrigation, in others it is so high as to make the water unsafe even for human or animal consumption. Conditions are comparatively worse, with respect to both quantity and quality, in the area northeast of the Uebi Scebeli (Mudugh and Migiurtinia), but even in the rest of the country—except in the immediate vicinity of the Juba—the supply of water is scarce, erratic and unpredictable.[47]

The scarcity of water plays a crucial role in shaping the way of life of the Somalis. Much of the intertribal fighting that breaks out every now and then is caused by disputes over water rights.[48] Whether a Somali pursues a nomadic, seminomadic, or sedentary way of life depends in large part upon how much water is available in any one place and the distance between water holes. The availability of water also determines the composition of herds. Cattle, all of them of the zebu type, are apt to predominate only in the most favorable areas. Though several drought-resistant varieties have been developed locally, Somali cattle must nevertheless have water at least every two days during drought periods. Where water is less abundant, herds usually consist of camels, goats and sheep, and in the driest parts of the country only camels are raised, since camels can go without water for as long as twelve days in a period of drought.[49]

The scarcity of water explains the preference for herding as an occupation as well as the hoarding of livestock. To obtain the means of subsistence the majority of the population must resort either to farming or to herding, since fishing and hunting provide only limited possibilities. Centuries of experience have taught the Somalis that tilling the soil in a country where water supplies are unreliable affords far less economic security than

[47] T. P. Ahrens, *A Reconnaissance Ground-Water Survey of Somalia, East Africa*, Rome, 1953, pp. 47–81. The data on rainfall cited in the text are based on A. Fantoli, *Carte Pluviometriche della Somalia*, Rome, 1955.

[48] Bozzi and Triulzi, *op. cit.*, p. 288.

[49] U.N. Doc. T/1296, pp. 6–7; Bozzi and Triulzi, *op. cit.*, p. 269.

stock-raising. When crops fail because of a drought, as frequently happens, there is little the Somali farmer can do to avoid starvation. While drought poses the most serious threat, there are also other hazards with which the Somali farmer must cope, such as insects, birds, and rodents, since any one of these may damage, if not completely ruin, the crops on which he depends for sustenance. In an environment as harsh and as primitive as that of Somalia, therefore, the man who makes his livelihood by cultivating the soil leads a most insecure existence. To be sure, the possibility of averting the threat of famine by storing food when harvests are abundant has not been overlooked by the Somali farmer, who has developed a primitive, though in many ways ingenious, technique of storing cereals underground. Nevertheless this type of storage does not provide an adequate solution to the problem of economic insecurity, in the first place because a substantial part of the stored grain is likely to spoil, and secondly because abundant harvests in most areas are relatively rare.[50] In most instances, therefore, crop failure means starvation for the Somali farmer, and nothing but external aid can save him from this cruel fate.

The herder is in a different position. He too has reason to fear droughts, for his animals must have water. Compared with the farmer, however, he has the advantage of mobility; in the event of drought he and his herd can travel as far as may be necessary to reach a new well or water hole. But the herder must face certain other problems. During a drought his animals will usually give no milk and in order to support himself he will be forced to slaughter a certain number of them, thereby reducing the size of the herd. Moreover, the herder cannot always foresee how far he may have to travel to reach a new source of water and pasturage. The journey may be long and many of his animals, because of their unequal ability to endure hardship, may

[50] See Chapter IV.

succumb on the way. Furthermore, animal disease may take its toll. Somali livestock is plagued by many diseases, such as rinderpest, pleuropneumonia, hoof-and-mouth disease, which affect cattle; trypanosomiasis, which affects both cattle and camels; hemorrhagic septicaemia, which affects goats; and a large variety of parasitic diseases which affect all types of live-stock.[51] Hence, if the herder is to reach his destination safely and still have enough animals left with which to rebuild his herd, he must have a large number of them to begin with. This is why he is so anxious to hoard livestock. The larger his herd, the stronger is the probability that a sufficient number of animals will survive to enable him to complete the journey successfully.

This preoccupation with economic security is clearly shown in the herder's consumption habits. In order to maximize the utilization of livestock resources for subsistence purposes without unnecessarily reducing the size of the herd, the greatest emphasis is placed on dairy products while meat consumption is minimized. The same reasoning lies behind the reluctance to sell animals with breeding capabilities. Thus in his quest for future security the Somali herder is willing to forego many present satisfactions, and there is nothing to suggest the improvidence attributed to him by the cattle-complex theory and many popular beliefs. Social attitudes such as contempt for agricultural pursuits and the prestige that is attached to the ownership of large herds merely reflect the intense concern with economic security. Given the herder's greater chances for the latter, it is certainly not difficult to understand why farming should be held in low esteem or why the owner of a large herd should be envied by his fellow men.

The pattern of seasonal variation in livestock prices on the Mogadiscio market, the only domestic market for which money prices are available, provides additional evidence of the herder's

---

[51] U.N. Doc. ST/TAA/J/Somaliland/R.1, pp. 139-40.

concern with security. During the dry season of *gilal*, that is, from January to March, or whenever there is a drought, livestock sales fall and prices rise; with the return of more favorable weather conditions, sales pick up again and prices drop. In other words, the supply curve for livestock on the Mogadiscio market shifts to the left whenever drought hits the country.[52]

Apart from security considerations, the Somali has no particular reason to dislike agriculture.[53] Nomadic pastoralism is in fact carried on only in those regions where the environment offers no suitable alternative. Where it is possible to grow crops for a few months in the year, the herder is also a part-time farmer and the movements of men and stock acquire the more regular pattern of transhumance. Sedentary agriculture is practiced wherever the environment permits it, though this does not mean that the settled farmer has no interest in raising stock. So long as he can afford it, he will always try to maintain as many animals as possible, as a precaution against unforeseeable emergencies. The only exception to this is to be found in certain riverine areas which are so heavily infested with tse-tse flies that no stock can be kept because of the danger of trypanosomiasis.

As for the argument that concern with the number of animals in disregard of considerations of quality constitutes uneconomic behavior, it can only be said that the argument is based on a

[52] W. W. Worzella and A. L. Musson, *Proposed Program for Agricultural Technical Assistance for Somalia*, USOM/Italy, 1954, p. 7.

[53] Maugini, *Flora ed Economia Agraria degli Indigeni delle Colonie Italiane di Diretto Dominio*, Rome, 1931, p. 155; R. Di Lauro, *Il Giuba Economico*, Turin, 1931, p. 16; A. Folco, "L'Agricoltura Indigena della Somalia Italiana," *Atti del Secondo Congresso di Studi Coloniali*, VI, Florence, 1936, p. 969. That the Somali herder, in point of fact, does not particularly object to farming except where security considerations are involved is also borne out by recent press reports. Many nomadic herders are reportedly settling in areas where modern irrigated farms have been set up under the Italian Administration's Seven Year Development Plan. See *Corriere della Somalia*, December 20, 1957. For an analysis of the Plan see Chapter VII.

mistaken notion that physical productivity is the sole test of economic efficiency. Technical efficiency, as has been often pointed out, does not mean the same thing as economic efficiency. The latter refers to an organization of production which minimizes the use of the relatively scarcer resources in the effort to achieve certain given objectives. Technical efficiency may coincide with economic efficiency, but this will always depend upon individual circumstances as well as upon individual goals within a particular society.

The hoarding of livestock in Somalia is therefore explained chiefly by a desire for security. The explanation resembles in many ways that offered by Keynes in his discussion of liquidity-preference arising out of a precautionary motive. But the analogy with liquidity-preference must not be pressed too far. For Somali livestock is not money, and if it changes hands on the occasion of marriage or when compensation for damages must be made, it is because, in addition to the fact that it is easily transferred, it represents the most valuable asset in an environment where economic security, in the most fundamental sense of the term, is so difficult to achieve that it becomes the final end of economic activity.

THE OBSTACLES TO STRUCTURAL CHANGE

UP TO this point the explanation of livestock accumulation has been based on two assumptions: a primitive level of technological knowledge and a low level of domestic capital. These assumptions are realistic only if the discussion is limited to the situation which existed in Somalia before the country fell under European influence. The explanation is therefore incomplete, since it fails to take into account the persistence of the phenomenon of livestock accumulation in modern times, when the methods of a superior Western technology are available and the supply of capital can be augmented from external sources. Surveys conducted by technical experts indicate that it is possible to increase the quantity and improve the quality of both surface water and ground water by a variety of means, such as, for example, the construction of off-channel storage facilities and the drilling of deep wells. It is also possible, through inoculations and other means, to cut stock losses resulting from tropical diseases. The execution of a vast program of water improvement and animal disease control would of course require substantial amounts of foreign capital, but the latter can be obtained, provided that there is sufficient economic justification for diverting it from other uses.

Other factors being equal, the implementation of such a program would lead to an increase in the supply of livestock to the limit of the carrying capacity of the land. An increase in water supply would create but limited additional opportunities in agriculture for obtaining the means of subsistence, since much of the new water supply, particularly that obtained from the underflow, could be used only for watering stock. In terms of economic security, there would still be no suitable alternative to the hoarding of livestock, and the incentive to hoard as many head as possible would thus remain strong. At present the scarcity of water acts as a Malthusian check on the increase of livestock population; grazing land appears to be relatively abundant, and though there is evidence of overgrazing in some parts of the country, this is due to a temporary maldistribution of stock in relation to the amount of natural pasture rather than to a general shortage of the latter.[54] Should the supply of water be increased, however, a process would be set in motion which in time would cause pressure of livestock population on the land. Measures to combat animal diseases would only help to

[54] M. Klemme, *Forestry and Range Management Survey, Somalia, East Africa*, USOM/Italy, 1957, pp. 20–21.

speed up this process toward an eventual reversal of the scarcity ratio between land and water. Overgrazing would then cause the land to deteriorate and this would ultimately bring about a contraction in the supply of livestock. The net effect of this process would therefore be the substitution of one Malthusian check for another, without any appreciable gain in security or other economic advantages for the herder.[55]

In the event of an increase in the supply of livestock, compulsory destocking may be resorted to as a means of preventing the impairment of grazing land. But compulsory destocking seems justified only if there is no alternative course of action, since it is basically wasteful and, in addition, is likely to be resisted by the pastoralist. A more rational approach to the problem is to raise the level of commercialization of livestock resources.

At this point it seems desirable to prevent a possible misunderstanding as to the relation between the need for adjusting livestock numbers to the carrying capacity of the land, and marketing. It is not reasonable to view the conservation of natural resources, despite its obvious importance, as the basic criterion for a policy of marketing livestock products, although this is what is implied in many statements and discussions about livestock problems in East Africa. Notions of this kind are highly misleading with regard to the nature of the changes entailed in the transition from subsistence to market activities. They emphasize the importance of marketing as a means of removing a surplus number of animals from the land and give the impression that the herder, once his stock has been reduced to some extent, will be left free to carry on his subsistence and other activities more or less as he did before. From this point of view the only

[55] Experiences in Kenya and elsewhere suggest that a long-term process along the lines indicated above is something more than a purely theoretical possibility. See *Report of the Kenya Land Commission*, 1934 (Cmd. 4556), pp. 494–500.

change would be a quantitative change, though not necessarily a significant one, in the commercialization of livestock resources. Actually, the transition to market activities would involve a highly complex process, requiring numerous changes in production functions not only in the pastoral sector but throughout the whole economy. A project for marketing frozen beef, for instance, would call for the establishment of refrigerating plants, which might give rise to a diversion of capital from the plantation sector and of labor from the same sector or from indigenous agriculture; in turn this might cause a decline in output of food and other commodities, thereby providing an impetus for new imports, etc. The transition to market activities would therefore entail a transformation of the whole economy, that is, economic development in Schumpeter's sense of the term. The salient feature of this revolutionary process is not the conservation of natural resources, but the fact that it makes possible a steep rise in social income, though the two objectives are certainly compatible. In other words, it is the possibility of attaining a higher level of income that constitutes an appropriate criterion for economic development, while the protection of natural resources represents only an incidental benefit.[56]

A higher level of commercialization of livestock resources therefore appears greatly desirable. Certainly it would require many changes in the conditions of supply, such as, for example, organization of range management along modern lines, improved breeding practices, and establishment of new processing industries. Many technical and organizational problems would thus have to be faced, but none of them, at least in principle, would seem to be insoluble. A substantial amount of capital would also be needed, but its availability would largely depend upon the demand for it, which in turn would depend upon the

[56] On this point see also *Report of the East Africa Royal Commission,* 1955 (Cmd. 9475), pp. 293–312.

state of final demand, that is, the demand for livestock and livestock products. The latter is, therefore, of crucial importance.

As previously noted, the domestic demand for livestock products is limited by low purchasing power. The same is true of the demand for these products in other underdeveloped areas, such as the Arabian peninsula and the adjacent African territories.[57] There is also the fact that the neighboring East African countries have large livestock supplies of their own and are faced with a similar problem of finding outlets for them. It remains to inquire, then, whether developed countries have anything to offer in the way of demand for animal products that would justify exports from Somalia on a large scale.

It has long been argued that Italy provides a logical market for Somali meat products.[58] In Italy demand for meat exceeds domestic output by a considerable margin, and the gap is regularly filled by imports. Since meat is scarce in Italy while cattle are abundant in Somalia, the obvious thing to do, it is maintained, is to organize exports of Somali meat to Italy. If this has not been done until now, it is because regulations in force in all European countries prohibit the importation of meat from areas in which rinderpest and hoof-and-mouth disease are known to be prevalent. In Italy this prohibition applies primarily to fresh and frozen meats, regulations being somewhat less stringent with regard to the importation of canned products. So long,

---

[57] U.N. Doc. T/1200, pp. 32–33.

[58] A. Cortinois, "Le Ricchezze Naturali della Nostra Somalia," *Agricoltura Coloniale,* II (1908); F. Martoglio, "Dell'Allevamento del Bestiame e del Suo Trasporto in Italia," *Atti del Secondo Congresso degli Italiani all'Estero,* I, Rome, 1911; L. Cufino, "Il Commercio della Somalia Italiana," *Esplorazione Commerciale,* XXVII (April, 1912), p. 6; A. Mallarini, "La Somalia Italiana Meridionale in Rapporto all'Economia Nazionale," *Atti del Convegno Nazionale Coloniale,* Naples, 1917; U. Ferretti, "Può in Somalia Sorgere una Industria delle Carni?", *Rivista del Freddo,* XVI (1930); Bettini, "Problemi Zootecnici della Somalia," pp. 263–64.

therefore, as these regulations are enforced against Somalia, only canned meat can be exported. But the demand for canned meat, though it exists, is smaller by far than that for products in fresh or frozen form, and consequently it does not alone provide an adequate basis for a full-scale mobilization of Somali livestock resources.

Although the Italian ban on imports from areas affected by rinderpest and hoof-and-mouth disease rules out any immediate possibility of large-scale meat imports from Somalia, it would be wrong to assume that the presence of animal disease is the most serious obstacle. Much headway has already been made in the fight against rinderpest, and it is generally agreed that there exist no major scientific problems to block further progress.[59] The battle against animal disease can be won, but success in this field would still leave many and complex economic questions to be resolved before there could be any genuine hope of linking Somali supply with Italian demand for meat products. The main problem here is one of prices and costs, not the technical conditions of production.

The mere fact that the demand for meat exceeds domestic output does not by itself warrant the conclusion that there is a large potential market in Italy for Somali livestock products. Until 1951 Italian domestic output was supplemented by imports primarily from Uruguay and Argentina; since then New Zealand, France, and Denmark have become more important as sources of supply.[60] The Italian market for meat products of foreign origin is therefore highly competitive, and if Somali producers are to enter it they must be able to land goods of certain types and

[59] Corfitzen and Kinzy, *op. cit.*, pp. 15–16; C. L. McColloch, *Livestock Survey, Somalia, East Africa*, USOM/Italy, 1957, p. 10.

[60] E. Bartolozzi, "Il Fabbisogno Italiano di Prodotti Agrari Subtropicali e Tropicali," *Rivista di Agricoltura Subtropicale e Tropicale*, L (1956), pp. 204–205.

qualities in Italy at prices that will cover costs of production and transfer and still be no higher than those offered by competitors.

It is not possible to estimate the cost of production that would obtain under these circumstances, although past and current prices on the Mogadiscio market are sometimes cited in support of the view that the cost of production would be low. In point of fact, these prices are not relevant. The organization of meat exports on a large scale would necessitate changes in production functions along lines which cannot be foreseen. Even if one were to make the utterly unrealistic assumption that present supply functions would continue to prevail, it would still be impossible to estimate the prices that would emerge with a change in quantities traded, since too little is known about the form, slope, and behavior of present supply functions. While the cost of production cannot be calculated in advance, one can, however, assume that, as a matter of probability, it will not fall below that of Italy's present suppliers. The best that can be hoped for is that it will be equal, though even this seems doubtful in view of the country's general state of underdevelopment.

As for the cost of transfer, it is practically certain to be high. Present marketing, transport, and port facilities in Somalia fall far short of what would be needed for handling a large volume of trade.[61] To develop them would require enormous expenditures, a large part of which would inevitably be translated into direct and indirect costs of transfer.[62] Hence the total cost of

[61] U.N. Doc. T/1296, p. 71; McColloch, *op. cit.*, p. 8.

[62] The following illustration should help to make clear what is meant here by direct and indirect transfer costs:

Let us assume that the government decides to build a road so as to facilitate the transport of meat products. There are three ways by which it can finance construction and maintenance. It can institute a user tax, rely on other types of taxes, or resort to inflationary financing. If a user tax is chosen, a direct cost will be incurred by the meat industry to the extent that it makes use of the road. If some other type of tax is imposed, the

transfer, which must include sea transport charges and Suez Canal tolls, would be high. When added to the cost of production, it would raise the price of Somali meat products to a level which would deny them access to the Italian market.

From all that has been said thus far, it follows that the conditions of demand necessary for the development of Somalia's livestock resources do not exist. For such conditions to arise in the future, either domestic purchasing power must increase, or purchasing power in some other underdeveloped country must increase, or demand prices for livestock products in developed countries must rise above present levels and to an extent sufficient to cover production and transfer costs.

It has been suggested that even if demand were to improve, commercialization would be thwarted by the Somali herder's well-known reluctance to sell livestock.[63] The possibility of this, it must be admitted, cannot be excluded a priori. Custom exerts a strong influence upon human behavior, and it is entirely possible that it will continue to guide the herder's actions even under changing economic conditions. Yet one may doubt that this influence would manifest itself for very long, if at all, should the pressure exerted by demand forces prove to be strong. This at least is what wartime experiences in Kenya and Uganda, when the presence of Commonwealth armed forces caused the demand for meat and other livestock products to soar, seem to indicate. Not only did African herders show themselves willing to sell then, but they actually exhibited such zeal that the Uganda Veterinary Department complained about "overselling." [64] Evidently these

burden of taxation will be shared by different industries, but a part of it will fall upon the meat industry itself and to this extent it will represent an indirect cost of transfer. And if inflationary financing is resorted to, an indirect cost of transfer will be incurred in the form of higher labor and other production costs.

[63] Maugini, "Lineamenti dell'Economia Rurale della Somalia," p. 219.

[64] Batten, *op. cit.*, Part I, p. 73. See also *Report of the East Africa Royal Commission*, 1955 (Cmd. 9475), pp. 303–304.

herders were quick to recognize that the high income levels which are possible in a market economy would give them a far greater measure of security than that which they could achieve by hoarding stock. Should an improvement in the conditions of demand ever materialize, there is no reason to believe that the response of Somali herders would be slower than that of their counterparts in Kenya and Uganda. But until such an improvement comes about, there are substantial reasons why Somali herders should wish to continue hoarding stock. It may also be added that a policy aiming to persuade livestock owners to sell seems undesirable, inasmuch as under these circumstances it can only succeed in arousing false hopes and in inducing the owners to take certain steps that might jeopardize the small measure of security which they now enjoy.

Ultimately, then, it is the level of final demand which represents the most serious obstacle to structural change. For in the absence of large and regular markets, the demand for capital tends to remain low, and this in turn tends to discourage changes in production functions. The pastoral economy is therefore unable to take much advantage of the possibilities opened up by modern science and technology, and this explains the preservation of an old structure, the principal characteristics of which are limited commercialization and accumulation of livestock.

[CHAPTER IV]

Indigenous Agriculture

LIKE THE activity of the pastoral sector, indigenous agriculture is characterized by production for direct consumption and a limited degree of commercialization. It is practiced in riverine areas, where the presence of the tse-tse fly makes it impossible to raise livestock. Elsewhere it represents an activity essentially subsidiary to herding.

The indigenous agriculture sector compares unfavorably with the plantation sector in terms of income, and while this is also true of the pastoral sector, agriculture has the added disadvantage of providing little in the way of security. Of the three sectors that make up Somalia's economy, indigenous agriculture is the weakest. Some of the principal reasons for this weakness will become apparent in the ensuing discussion of the two most salient features of indigenous agriculture: the under-utilization of land and the indebtedness of the farmer.

Under-utilization of Land

From the standpoint of cultivation methods used and types of crops raised, it is useful to distinguish between rain-fed and flood-irrigated agriculture. Rain-fed agriculture is practicable wherever the soil is of a quality that makes it suitable for cultivation and precipitation attains an annual mean of not less than 12 inches.[1] In Somalia it is concentrated primarily in the upland region that lies between the Uebi Scebeli and the Juba, though it is practiced on a small scale in many other parts of the country. Flood-irrigated agriculture, on the other hand, is limited to farmlands in the immediate vicinity of the two rivers.

Different techniques of flood irrigation are used in the Uebi Scebeli area and near the Juba, owing to different topographical conditions. The level of the Uebi Scebeli, unlike the Juba's, is higher than that of the adjoining plain. The Uebi Scebeli rises in flood twice a year during periods which coincide with the rainy seasons of southern Ethiopia; whenever this occurs the Somali farmer simply breaks the banks of the river, causing its waters to overflow into the neighboring plain. Some of the flood water infiltrates the soil and the rest is eventually lost through evaporation. Crops are then planted and brought to maturity with the aid of additional rainfall. Near the Juba the same method of irrigation cannot be used, because the ground there lies above the level of the river. Near the river's middle and lower course, however, there are a number of fertile depressions, called *desheks* by the Somalis. The *desheks* are connected with the river by *fars*, or channels, most of which appear to be of natural origin. During flood stage the Juba rises to a level six to twelve feet above the bottom of the *desheks*, thereby causing some water

[1] Annual Report of the Italian Government to the United Nations on Somalia, 1953, p. 119.

to flow through the *fars* and into the *desheks*. When the native farmer thinks that a sufficient amount of water has entered the *deshek*, he closes the *fars* by piling up soil, debris or other material against them. At the end of the flood period he reopens them, thereby allowing some of the water in the *deshek* to flow back into the river, the level of which by this time has once again fallen below that of the *deshek*. Whatever water may still be left in the *deshek* is either soaked up by the ground or gradually evaporated by the sun. Crops are planted as soon as the ground is sufficiently dry and, as is done on the fields near the Uebi Scebeli, are brought to maturity with the aid of additional rainfall.

In the irrigated areas a large variety of crops, such as durra, sesame, beans, gourds, and potatoes, are grown, but the principal crop is corn. Cereals are similarly favored in rain-fed areas, but low average precipitation restricts the choice to those crops which can be raised by dry-land farming methods. Attempts to raise corn usually meet with little success, since the water requirements of corn are relatively high. The principal crop in these areas is durra, a variety of sorghum well known for its drought-resistant qualities. Small amounts of beans are also grown and attempts are made to raise other food crops from time to time, though seldom with any notable measure of success.

The physical productivity of the land appears to be generally low, although yields are said to vary greatly from year to year. Little is available in the way of accurate statistics, but recent estimates place the yield in rain-fed areas at about 900 pounds of durra per acre during periods of normal rainfall and that on flood-irrigated farms at about 1,100 pounds of durra or corn.[2] The low yield per unit of land in rain-fed areas is to a large extent due to the use of extensive methods of cultivation.

[2] E. Conforti, "Aspetti del Problema Idrico nell'Agricoltura Somala," *Rivista di Agricoltura Subtropicale e Tropicale*, XLVII (1953), pp. 230–37.

The farmer cannot determine the extent of future precipitation, because rainfall is not only low on the average but also extremely irregular; he is therefore inclined to scatter seeds over as large an area as possible, so as to minimize the risk of total failure.[3] Yields on irrigated farms, though they appear to be slightly better than on rain-fed lands, are also unsatisfactory, but this is accounted for, at least in part, by difficulties encountered in the regulation of flood waters. For once the fields have been inundated they may remain submerged for a long time. The *desheks* of the Juba, for instance, may remain submerged for periods ranging anywhere from two weeks to six months.[4] The presence of excessive quantities of stagnant water affects crops adversely in more than one way, but particularly through the rapid growth of plant parasites and diseases which it tends to encourage.

A more fundamental reason for the low productivity of the land is the lack of complementary factors of production, especially labor. With a larger supply of manpower it would be possible to increase the output of indigenous agriculture by a more intensive utilization of land, particularly in flood-irrigated areas, where environmental conditions appear to be somewhat better than on rain-fed lands. It would also be possible to bring more land into cultivation, since only a small proportion of the total amount of arable land available is now in use.[5]

The only major source of manpower available in Somalia is the pastoral sector, but indigenous agriculture is unable to draw on it to any considerable extent largely because of the lack of incentives. The large element of economic insecurity that stems

[3] R. Tozzi, "Programma di Attività per Incrementare l'Agricoltura Somala," *ibid.*, p. 253.

[4] Conforti, *op. cit.*, p. 238.

[5] Near the Juba, for instance, the Somalis are rarely able to bring more than a small proportion of the land available in the *desheks* under cultivation, notwithstanding the high fertility of the soil. AFIS, *Sopraluogo dell'Ispettore per l'Agricoltura e la Zootecnia nella Regione del Basso Giuba,* 1954 (mimeographed).

from the scarcity of water on rain-fed lands and from the excess of water on flood-irrigated farms makes indigenous agriculture so unattractive that the herder is usually unwilling to give up his present occupation for it.

To some extent it might be possible to make up for the shortage of labor by a greater use of capital equipment. The introduction of more modern equipment and techniques would undoubtedly help to raise output, since the agricultural implements that the farmer now uses are of the most rudimentary type. But there are limits to the possibilities of substituting capital for labor in agriculture, and these limits are particularly narrow where agricultural activities are carried on primarily for the sake of direct consumption.

FARMER INDEBTEDNESS

To THE native farmer the greatest problem is to find some way of overcoming the threat of famine posed by frequent crop failures. Within the limits of his knowledge and means, the farmer has done his best to solve the problem, but without much success. The idea of storing cereals when harvests are good has certainly occurred to him. Methods of storing grain underground have been developed and are widely used today. Unfortunately, grain storage has provided only a partial and none too satisfactory way of meeting the problem of security. The reasons are essentially technical in nature.

The usual practice is to dig a shallow pit in the ground and line it with corn stalks or other fiber residues. The grain—chiefly corn and durra—is then placed in the pit, covered with fiber mats and several feet of soil. Grain stored in this way can be preserved for many months, even years, but the high moisture content of corn and durra inevitably causes a certain amount of spoilage.[6]

[6] R. F. Germann, *Somalia Grain Study*, USOM/Italy, 1953.

According to an American expert, the spoilage that results from excessive moisture content varies between 25 and 50 per cent of the quantity stored.[7] Another and even more serious disadvantage of underground storage is the possibility of damage by insects and rodents. So long as the pit remains unopened and provided that it is made airtight, the grain will be protected by the absence of oxygen and the presence of carbon dioxide. Once the pit is opened, however, insects and rodents will begin their work at once and cause immense damage in a short time.[8]

Frequently, then, the native farmer's ability to survive depends upon the possibility of receiving aid from the outside. This contrasts sharply with common notions about the nature of a subsistence economy. For it is generally assumed that the poverty inherent in a subsistence economy is compensated for to some extent by a high degree of self-sufficiency. Somalia's indigenous agriculture, however, is gravely deficient on both counts.

The distressing situation in which the farmer often finds himself puts him at the mercy of Somali and Arab petty traders, who are willing to give him credit at exorbitant rates of interest. Ostensibly no interest is charged on loans, since all these traders are Mohammedans and Islam forbids lending at interest. Yet when full account is taken of the circumstances under which credit is made available, it becomes evident that the farmer is in fact compelled to bear a heavy interest burden. Whenever the petty trader extends credit to the hard-pressed farmer, he does it by offering him goods, chiefly foodstuffs and textiles, while the amount of the debt is fixed in terms of money. In keeping with his religious beliefs, the trader does not ask for interest and the farmer's obligation to repay is thus limited to the principal on the loan, which falls due at the next harvest; but since the farmer rarely has any money, he is more often than not compelled to

[7] H. Bross, *Somalia Grain Study*, USOM/Italy, 1954, p. 6.
[8] *Ibid.*, p. 3.

84

raise the money needed for repaying the loan by selling his crops to the trader from whom he had previously borrowed. Occasionally he may try to raise the necessary funds by selling his produce elsewhere, but in most instances he is reluctant to do so, lest he be cut off from customary credit facilities in the future. Under these circumstances the trader is largely in a position to dictate the prices of the goods he sells to as well as of those he buys from the hapless farmer. Needless to say, these prices differ considerably from the cash prices which obtain for the same goods on local markets. Indirectly, then, the trader does charge interest, the amount of which can be calculated as equal to the difference between market values and prices of goods sold to the farmer at the time the loan is advanced, plus the difference between market values and prices of goods bought from the farmer when the loan is repaid. The interest rate that is charged in this roundabout fashion has been estimated by one source as ranging between 50 and 100 per cent.[9]

It is of course easy to criticize the petty trader for indulging in what might be called, as indeed they have been, "usurious" practices. Yet it should be borne in mind that the petty trader is able to exact a high rate of interest only so long as nobody else is willing to offer better terms. The farmer, lacking proper collateral, has no access to commercial banks. Besides, the risk of lending in such cases is much greater than that which commercial banks or similar institutions can be expected to assume. Were it not for the petty trader's willingness to gamble for a large reward, the position of the native farmer would soon become untenable.

More objectionable than the high rate of interest is the indirect method by which it is charged and collected. The farmer has no possibility of knowing how much he really owes to the trader (nor does the latter, for that matter); nor can he calculate

[9] R. Onor, *La Somalia Italiana*, Turin, 1925, p. 88.

how and when he will be able to rid himself of debts. Should a harvest turn out to be more abundant than on a previous occasion, the farmer would gain little, since he would be pressured by the trader to sell his crops at lower prices. As a result the farmer is kept in a state of almost chronic indebtedness, which has a thoroughly depressing effect on the growth of savings in indigenous agriculture.

The high rate of interest and the chronic indebtedness of the farmer thus testify to the basic weakness of indigenous agriculture. Output is at too low a level and too irregular to permit indigenous agriculture to play a major role in the economy of Somalia. The low level of output, as previously pointed out, is in the main due to the lack of co-operant factors of production—primarily labor, and to some extent capital.

[CHAPTER V]

The Plantation Economy

THE MARKET economy of Somalia revolves around the activities of plantations, most of which are owned or controlled by Italians. The plantations are concentrated near the rivers and, in view of the unreliability of rainfall, are almost entirely dependent upon irrigation. Bananas, cotton, and sugar cane are the principal crops grown. The first two are produced for export, while the third is intended for sale on the domestic market. The aim of this chapter is to analyze the special problems to which the production of each of these crops gives rise.

THE PRODUCTION OF BANANAS UNDER MONOPSONISTIC INFLUENCE

THE PRODUCTION of bananas is in the hands of a number of Italian and a few Somali concessionaires, who have pooled

87

their resources to form three associations: *Società Anonima Co-operativa Agricola di Genale* (SACA), *Anonima Cooperativa Coltivatori Afgoi* (ACCA), and *Società Agricoltori Giuba* (SAG). SACA and ACCA plantations are concentrated near the Uebi Scebeli, at Genale and Afgoi, respectively, while SAG plantations are located near the Juba.

SACA plantations, as Table 13 shows, play a dominant role in the production of bananas. The reasons for this are partly historical. Before 1925 the Juba formed the border between Kenya and Somalia, and the Uebi Scebeli was the only river with both banks within Somali territory; initially, therefore, Italian efforts to develop irrigated agriculture along commercial lines were concentrated for the most part in the plain adjoining the Uebi Scebeli. By the time the Trans-Juba was annexed to Somalia, following the conclusion of a treaty between Great Britain and Italy, much labor and capital had already been invested at Genale. The development of a plantation system near the Juba did not begin until the late thirties and was soon interrupted by the outbreak of the Second World War; subsequent events did not permit continuation of prewar policies, and although activities on the plantations near the Juba were resumed with the return of peace, Genale retained its leading role in the production of bananas. As for ACCA, its entry into this line of production is a relatively recent development. For many years Italian growers at Afgoi had concentrated on garden vegetables and fruits to satisfy the demand for these products among Europeans living in nearby Mogadiscio, the country's capital, but they were faced with a severe economic crisis when the size of Mogadiscio's European population, both military and civilian, was substantially reduced following the establishment of trusteeship. The crisis lasted until the end of 1952, when, for want of a better alternative, Afgoi growers turned to the cultivation of bananas.[1]

[1] G. Rocchetti, "La Bananicoltura della Somalia," *Rivista di Agricoltura Subtropicale e Tropicale,* L (1956), p. 188.

The Plantation Economy

Less than one-fifth of the associations' total land holdings is devoted to bananas (Table 13). Many other crops are grown, chiefly cotton, peanuts, corn, sisal, and grapefruit, but compared with bananas they yield negligible earnings.

TABLE 13

RELATIVE IMPORTANCE OF PRODUCERS' ASSOCIATIONS IN THE
PRODUCTION AND EXPORT OF BANANAS, 1955

	SACA	ACCA	SAG	TOTAL
Number of concessions	156	38	41	235
Total land holdings *(thousands of acres)*	70	13	29	112
Acreage devoted to bananas *(thousands of acres)*	14	2	4	20
Acreage under bananas in bearing *(thousands of acres)*	10	1	4	15
Output *(thousands of tons)*	63	7	24	94
Exports *(thousands of tons)*	35	5	14	54

Sources: U.N. Doc. T/1296; G. Rocchetti, "La Bananicoltura della Somalia," *Rivista di Agricoltura Subtropicale e Tropicale*, L (1956).

The only type of banana grown on the plantations is *Juba nana,* a local strain of the dwarf variety known as Cavendish or *Musa sinensis.* Because of its greater ability to withstand strong winds, it is better suited to Somali conditions than the tall variety, called *Gros Michel* or *Musa sapientum,* which is grown in West Africa and Latin America. It is also less susceptible to Panama, Sikatoga and other cryptogamic diseases. In one important respect, however, it compares unfavorably with the *Gros Michel:* it bruises easily, because of its thin and delicate skin.[2]

Somali bananas are grown primarily for export to Italy. Domestic sales are negligible and the only other exports consist of occasional small shipments to Aden. The Somali banana industry is thus almost entirely dependent upon access to the Italian market. On the average, it meets about four-fifths of Italy's

[2] Rocchetti, *op. cit.,* pp. 165–75.

annual demand for bananas, the balance being made up of imports from French Guinea (the present Republic of Guinea) and the Canary Islands.[3]

The chief weakness of the industry is its inability to meet competition. In 1955, for example, bananas from Guinea and the Canary Islands were landed in Italy at about $154 per ton c.i.f., or roughly two-thirds of the comparable price for Somali bananas.[4] If it is at all possible for Somali producers to sell on the Italian market under these conditions, it is only because they form a part of an intricate and cumbersome network of institutional arrangements at the center of which lies an agency of the Italian Government, *Azienda Monopolio Banane* (AMB).

The mechanism of trade and distribution of Somali bananas may be briefly outlined as follows:

The quantity and f.o.b. price of Somali bananas to be purchased by Italy are fixed in advance by AMB, on the basis of contracts with the producers' associations in Somalia. The latter then agree among themselves on the quota to be furnished by each association.[5] After delivery at Somali ports, bananas are transported to Italy in freighters hired by AMB and sold to licensed wholesale distributors at a price which is designed to cover (1) the c.i.f. price of the fruit, (2) the cost of land transport in Italy, (3) the administrative expenses of AMB, and (4) the "profit" of AMB, which in reality is an indirect tax imposed by the Italian Government and ultimately paid for by the consumer. The gross profits of wholesale and retail distributors make up the difference between this price and the retail price, the ceiling of which is fixed by AMB.

Somali producers are not able to meet Italian demand throughout the year. Irrigation on SACA and ACCA plantations is un-

---

[3] U.N. Doc. T/1296, p. 20.
[4] *Ibid.*, p. 27.
[5] In 1955 the quotas were: SACA 65%, ACCA 10%, SAG 25%.

even because the Uebi Scebeli, as already noted, runs dry for a few months every year; as a result production on these plantations, which contribute the largest proportion of exports, falls off during the summer.[6] The additional quantities needed to meet Italian demand are purchased by AMB from other sources, mainly Guinea and the Canary Islands, at c.i.f. prices which, as pointed out before, compare quite favorably with those for Somali bananas. Yet this has no effect on wholesale and retail prices because AMB absorbs the difference through a tariff which applies to all bananas of non-Somali origin.

The argument most frequently employed to justify the existence and operations of AMB is that Somalia's banana industry must be protected against stronger competitors if it is to have access to the Italian market. This, however, is not a wholly accurate view of the matter. No doubt the Somali banana industry could not function, at least for the time being, without some degree of protection in Italy, but the powers of AMB extend well beyond the needs of protectionist policy. If it were merely a question of affording protection to Somali producers, AMB could be dispensed with altogether; a preferential tariff would accomplish just as much, more simply and at a lower administrative cost. AMB is a powerful political institution, so powerful, in fact, that it is able to prevent any contact between foreign producers, including those of Somalia, and domestic consumers. By virtue of the monopoly power which it exerts over domestic traders, it is able to maintain a structure of wholesale and retail prices that are uniformly high and rigid; by virtue of the monopsony power which it exerts over producers in Somalia, it is able to limit the quantity which they may export. AMB is thus in a position to provide a sheltered market for Somali bananas and at the same time limit the total volume of Italian imports of bananas as well as fulfill certain fiscal objectives of the Italian

[6] Rocchetti, *op. cit.*, pp. 166–68.

Government. The simultaneous pursuit of these policies creates a situation in which the banana industry is guaranteed a profitable market, yet is prevented from expanding along lines which are vital if it is to achieve that degree of efficiency which would eventually permit it to compete on a free market.

This is not to say that AMB is wholly responsible for the excessively high cost of Somali bananas. Many other factors, some technical and some economic, contribute to the high cost. Nevertheless it is contended here that AMB policy plays a significant and perhaps even a decisive role in keeping the industry at an uneconomic level of operation. The basis for this contention should become clearer with a fuller exposition of the reasons for the high cost of Somali bananas.

In Table 14 the average c.i.f. price of bananas exported from

TABLE 14
AVERAGE COST OF SOMALI BANANAS PER TON EXPORTED, 1955

ITEM	U.S. $ EQUIV-ALENTS	Per Cent
1. Cost before cutting, less proceeds from local sales	53	21
2. Producer's profit, including wages of management	40	16
Cost ex plantation	93	37
3. Cutting and packing	5	2
4. Packing material	24	9
5. Land transport	5	2
6. Stevedoring	9	4
7. Export tax	7	3
8. Miscellaneous fees	7	3
9. Interest on working capital	1	—
10. Wastage during sea transport, loading and unloading	11	4
Cost f.o.b. Somali ports	162	64
11. Sea transport and Italian statistical tax	90	36
Cost c.i.f. Italian ports	252	100

Source: U.N. Doc. T/1296.

Somalia to Italy in 1955 is broken down into its major components. By reference to this table the principal factors which account for the c.i.f. price can be summarized as follows:

1. The cost of transfer takes the largest share of the c.i.f. price (about 63 per cent). To bring this price within the range of that offered by competitive producers (about $154 per ton) solely through economies in production, the ex-plantation price would have to fall to zero. It follows that there are only two ways to bring the c.i.f. price down to a competitive level: (a) through a substantial reduction in the cost of transfer, or (b) through some reduction in the cost of transfer together with economies in production. The second alternative obviously represents the more practical approach.

2. The largest item in the cost of transfer is sea transport. The World Bank mission that visited Somalia in 1956 estimated that sea transport from Somalia to Italy costs about 50 per cent more than from Guinea.[7] In part this is due to the necessity of paying Suez Canal tolls, but in part it is also due to inefficient organization. AMB-hired freighters make only a few trips yearly, sometimes leave Somali ports with less than a full load, and carry little or no cargo on the return voyage.[8]

3. Since Somali bananas bruise easily, they must be carefully packed to avoid excessive spoilage. Usually they are crated, and this explains the high cost of packing and packing material. Moreover, crating raises the cost of transport, both on land and on sea, because it adds to the space occupied by cargo and to the cargo's total weight. In recent years increasing use has been made of paper bags, in which the bananas are packed with the help of special machines. The new method tends to reduce packing and transport costs in some measure, although the gain is partially offset by greater spoilage.[9]

[7] U.N. Doc. T/1296, p. 22.
[8] *Ibid.*; G. F. Malagodi, *Linee Programmatiche per lo Sviluppo Economico e Sociale della Somalia*, Rome, 1953, p. 236.
[9] Rocchetti, *op. cit.*, pp. 177–78.

4. The fact that most roads in Somalia are unpaved makes for high land-transport costs, owing to excessive fuel consumption and wear and tear on trucks. Similarly, lack of modern port facilities makes for high stevedoring costs, because of the necessity of using lighters for loading and unloading cargo. Poor roads and inadequate ports also contribute to wastage and increase the need for careful packing.

5. The quantity to be exported under contract with AMB is allocated among and within the producers' associations on the basis of quotas arrived at in a more or less arbitrary fashion. This method of allocation is strongly encouraged by AMB's policy of imposing quantitative restrictions on Italian imports of bananas. To some extent it benefits the Somali banana industry by promoting closer collaboration among producers and thereby facilitating the achievement of certain economies of scale as well as the task of raising the substantial amounts of capital required to run and improve the plantations; on the other hand it hampers the industry's development along more rational lines by its failure to provide adequate incentives for individual producers to seek out more efficient methods of production.

6. There are wide seasonal fluctuations of output, owing to the preponderant role of the plantations near the Uebi Scebeli, which does not permit year-round utilization of its waters. More favorable conditions exist along the Juba, which is practically perennial, but the advantages to be derived from more uniform irrigation are offset in part by the relatively greater scarcity of native labor and by the greater distance from plantation to port. These considerations, plus the realization that much of the capital already invested in the land around Genale and Afgoi would be lost, have so far deterred relocation of the entire industry along the Juba, although some thought has been given to the advisability of such a move.[10]

[10] *Ibid.*, 89–90.

7. The problem of seasonal fluctuations of output that arises out of existing conditions of irrigation in Somalia is aggravated by seasonal fluctuations of demand in Italy. Italian demand for bananas is highest from April to October, whereas output per unit of land in Somalia is highest from November to March. The technical conditions of production are such that an increase in output during the months of high demand in Italy is possible only at lower yields per unit of land, that is, by bringing more land into cultivation and at the price of overproduction during the rest of the year.[11] Estimates of annual waste incurred through overproduction between November and March—that is, the excess of output over exports, excluding the minimal amounts sold domestically and those exported to Aden—vary between one-third and one-half of total output.[12] Overproduction thus raises the cost of production considerably and indirectly contributes to the high cost of transfer; for by exporting the entire crop it might be possible to achieve additional economies in sea transport (since it would then be easier to arrange for freighters to carry a full cargo, make more frequent trips, etc.) as well as in other transfer items. Overproduction is thus related in a significant way to demand fluctuations on the Italian market, and it is therefore a matter of considerable interest to inquire into the reasons for these fluctuations.

The consumption of bananas in Italy falls off every winter, when domestically produced citrus fruits are in season. If retail prices were to fall during this period, Italian consumers might be tempted to buy larger quantities of bananas; this, as we have seen, is impossible because of price control. AMB's policy of rigid maintenance of retail prices, reinforced by quantitative restrictions on imports, is thus intended to safeguard the interests of domestic citrus growers, who, it is claimed, fear that con-

[11] U.N. Doc. T/1296, pp. 24–26; Rocchetti, *op. cit.*, pp. 193–94.
[12] Malagodi, *op. cit.*, p. 235; Rocchetti, *op. cit.*, p. 179.

sumers would purchase bananas instead of oranges and tangerines should banana prices be allowed to fall.

In principle, it is conceivable that a decline in the price of bananas would cause the Italian consumer to substitute bananas for citrus fruits. It is equally conceivable that the consumer would keep expenditures on citrus fruits constant and take advantage of the lower price to increase his consumption of bananas. Economic theory gives no answer to the question as to which of the two alternatives would prevail in reality. Substitution may occur; that it will is far from certain.

It is clear that if the Italian market is to absorb the entire annual output of Somali bananas, the retail price must fall below the present level, but this does not mean that it must fall to a point where it will compare favorably with prices of citrus fruits. Indeed, such a situation is not likely to arise. If it were, the chance of a price decline resulting in substitution would be relatively greater.

A comparison of per capita consumption of bananas and citrus fruits in France, Spain, and Italy tends to support the view that lower banana prices might be expected to increase consumption in Italy without any significant detrimental repercussions on the citrus trade. Conditions in France and Spain are sufficiently similar to those in Italy to justify such a comparison, since both countries produce citrus fruits domestically and import bananas from their respective dependencies.[13]

As Table 15 shows, per capita consumption of bananas in Italy during 1952–1956 was considerably lower than in France

[13] Strictly speaking, France is an importer, not a producer, of citrus fruits. However, more than half of all the oranges and tangerines imported into France originate from countries within the franc zone (specifically, Algeria, Morocco, and Tunisia), Algeria alone supplying at least a third. See E. Dussert and P. Jouve, *Les Productions Fruitières dans la Zone Franc*, Paris, 1956. Legally, Algeria is a part of France, and for all practical purposes Algerian citrus production may be considered a part of France's domestic output.

TABLE 15

PER CAPITA CONSUMPTION, EXPRESSED IN LBS., OF BANANAS,
ORANGES, AND TANGERINES IN FRANCE, ITALY, AND SPAIN,
1952–1956

YEAR	BANANAS			ORANGES AND TANGERINES		
	France	Italy	Spain	France	Italy	Spain
1952	12.6	1.5	5.2	26.0	20.7	44.9
1953	12.5	1.6	2.8	27.7	22.0	2.0
1954	13.8	1.7	3.7	28.7	21.2	37.7
1955	13.6	2.0	5.2	33.2	25.4	10.7
1956	13.3	2.2	6.7	22.0	19.1	8.3
1952–1956 average	**13.2**	**1.8**	**4.7**	**27.5**	**21.7**	**20.7**

Source: Food and Agriculture Organization, *Yearbook of Food and Agricultural Statistics,* VIII, 1954, and XI, 1957, Rome.

and Spain. During this period Italy also lagged behind France in average per capita consumption of oranges and tangerines and led Spain by a margin so slim as to be almost negligible. Indeed, it may be said that Italy did poorly even in this last respect, if the difference in trade orientation between the two countries is taken into account. For the Italian citrus trade is directed primarily toward the home market, while the Spanish trade is organized chiefly for export (Table 16). Citrus fruits are one of Spain's principal earners of badly needed foreign exchange, and their

TABLE 16

EXPORTS OF ORANGES AND TANGERINES EXPRESSED AS A
PERCENTAGE OF OUTPUT, ITALY AND SPAIN, 1952–1956

YEAR	ITALY	SPAIN
1952	29.9	56.8
1953	29.0	97.4
1954	30.1	62.0
1955	23.9	87.6
1956	36.6	77.6
1952–1956 average	29.9	76.3

Source: Food and Agriculture Organization, *Yearbook of Food and Agricultural Statistics,* VIII, 1954, and XI, 1957, Rome.

export is actively encouraged by the government. As a consequence, domestic consumption of oranges and tangerines is limited to those quantities which, for one reason or another, do not find their way into foreign markets. This accounts for the sharp variations in Spain's annual domestic consumption.

It must therefore be concluded that a higher level of per capita consumption of bananas is compatible with a level of per capita consumption of citrus fruits higher or at least equal to that which is currently enjoyed in Italy. It may be argued that per capita consumption of both types of fruit is higher in France than in Italy because per capita income in the former is higher. But the argument loses much of its force when the Spanish case is also considered, since per capita income in Spain is lower than in Italy.[14]

With lower retail prices, it should therefore be possible for Somali banana producers to dispose of their winter surplus in Italy without necessarily hurting the interests of Italian citrus growers. Present AMB policy, however, precludes such a solution. An alternative, though less satisfactory, solution would be to sell the surplus on other foreign markets. Clearly, it would pay Somali producers to sell at any price above the cost of transfer rather than to let the fruit be completely wasted on the plantations. Unfortunately there are two major obstacles to this second solution: one is AMB control of all sea transport for bananas out of Somalia and the other is lack of adequate incentives for producers to increase their efficiency.[15] The lack of

---

[14] See C. P. Kindleberger, *Economic Development*, New York, 1958, p. 6.

[15] Since 1957 output per unit of land has been increased, and production costs correspondingly lowered, by planting banana trees at closer intervals than was previously believed possible. The new technique permits a closer adjustment of output to demand conditions in Italy and should therefore provide a partial solution to the problem of overproduction. Technical developments of this kind, however, do not affect the argument that by allowing market forces to determine Italian demand, the Somali banana industry would be in a position to increase its exports and lower c.i.f. prices.

incentives is the direct consequence of the present system of guaranteed profits.

It is thus patent that the difficulties which beset the Somali banana industry are chiefly due to the close ties which bind it to AMB. To explain the origin and development of these ties it is necessary to give a brief historical sketch of the conditions under which the industry was initially established.

Until 1929, the principal crop grown on plantations and exported from Somalia was cotton, but Italians had become interested in the possibility of raising bananas long before then. As far back as 1913, an Italian writer, A. Paoletti, had pointed out that environmental conditions in Somalia were highly favorable and that the cultivation of bananas had an important advantage over that of cotton in that it required a relatively small labor force.[16] But until 1926 bananas were grown largely on an experimental basis. With the collapse of the world market price of cotton in 1929, interest in bananas rose sharply and within a few years bananas became Somalia's chief export crop.

Banana exports to Italy began in 1927, in the face of stiff competition from producers in the Canary Islands. Despite lower production costs, producers in Somalia were at a definite disadvantage because of the longer distance over which the fruit had to be transported.[17] Nevertheless, producers in Somalia were confident that they would be able to improve their position in the long run. Similar difficulties had initially been experienced by

[16] "Il Valore Economico del Banano," *Agricoltura Coloniale*, VII (1913), pp. 281–97.

[17] B. Francolini, "Le Promesse della Somalia Italiana: Commercio Bananiero," *Illustrazione Coloniale*, XIII, No. 8 (1931), p. 35. Bananas usually spoil within 30 days from the time they are cut, but spoilage can be retarded by means of refrigeration. Hence Somali bananas, unlike those of the Canaries, must be transported to Europe in ships equipped with special refrigerating facilities. See G. Cavallini, "Gli Impianti Frigoriferi delle Nuovi Navi Bananiere della R. Azienda Monopolio Banane," *Rivista del Freddo*, XXIV (1938), p. 147.

banana growers in French West Africa, but were eventually overcome.[18]

Meanwhile, Somali producers demanded and obtained protection from the Italian Government. By a law passed in 1927 and amended in 1930, Italy imposed a tariff on all bananas of non-Somali origin.[19] In 1932 an even more drastic step was taken. The importation of bananas of non-Somali origin was prohibited, with one exception. Because of an earlier commercial agreement with Spain which was still in force, bananas from the Canaries were exempted from the provisions of the new law. The previously established tariff, however, still applied to them.[20]

Under the shield of these protectionist measures, the Somali industry made rapid progress. Output and exports soared within a few years. Overproduction was considerable but was gradually decreasing (Table 17). The cost of transport was also falling.

TABLE 17
PREWAR OUTPUT AND EXPORTS OF SOMALI BANANAS

YEAR	ACRES	Total Output (Tons)	Output Per Acre (Tons)	Exports (Tons)	Per Cent of Output Exported
1926	110	400	3.6	—	—
1927	130	600	4.6	5	0.8
1928	620	2,200	3.5	50	2.3
1929	930	3,300	3.5	230	7.0
1930	1,440	5,500	3.8	800	14.5
1931	3,050	11,000	3.6	1,400	12.7
1932	5,260	22,000	4.2	6,200	28.2
1933	6,530	28,000	4.3	9,600	34.3
1934	9,470	33,100	3.5	15,200	45.9
1935	9,880	38,600	3.9	15,700	40.6
1936	9,820	49,600	5.0	20,400	41.1
1937	—[a]	49,600	—[a]	24,900	50.2

Sources: L. Fioresi, "Le Banane e il Loro Commercio," *Rivista del Freddo* XXIII (1937); B. Conforti, *L'Esportazione delle Banane della Somalia Italiana dagli Inizi ad Oggi e Suoi Futuri Sviluppi*, Florence, 1939.
a = not available.

[18] Y. Henry, *Bananes et Ananas*, Paris, 1905.
[19] Francolini, *op. cit.*, p. 35.
[20] E. Cibelli, *Per il Traffico Bananiero Nazionale*, Rome, 1938, pp. 21–23.

Sea transport was at first provided by an Italian company, but producers later took advantage of a competitive offer by British and Swedish shipowners which enabled them to cut the cost of sea transport by about 40 per cent.[21]

In 1935, the Fascist Government created the *Regia Azienda Monopolio Banane* (RAMB). It gave RAMB the sole right to import bananas and sell them in Italy, as well as full control over their transport from Somalia. Seven Italian ships were put at RAMB's disposal for this purpose.

It was stated at the time that this move was justified on the ground that the ban on imports of bananas of non-Somali origin had created an opportunity for producers in Somalia to exploit Italian consumers by acting in concert. Through RAMB, it was claimed, a price policy could be pursued which would represent a compromise between the interests of Somali producers and those of Italian consumers. But the real reason was that the Fascist Government, partly as a reaction to the imposition of economic sanctions by the League of Nations, had decided in 1935 to embark on a policy of autarchy and centralization of economic activities under state direction. The creation of RAMB was just one of several measures taken to fulfill the goals of the new Fascist economic policy.[22] What needs to be emphasized in this regard is that the producers in Somalia had not solicited the creation of a state monopoly, an action which in all probability was inimical to their long-run interests. It was simply a case where, as one writer put it, the interests of the producers in Somalia had to yield before those of the Fascist State.[23]

The end of the Second World War found RAMB in process of liquidation, while the Somali banana industry was practically at a standstill. Shortly before the Italian Government assumed

[21] *Ibid.*, pp. 19–20.
[22] Cibelli, *op. cit.*, pp. 161–90.
[23] A. Brusa, "Il Traffico Bananiero, la RAMB e l'Autarchia," *Rassegna d'Oltremare*, VIII, No. 7 (1938).

its duties as administering authority for the trust territory of Somalia, it suddenly reactivated the banana monopoly, now known as AMB.[24]

Several reasons lay behind the Italian Government's decision. In the first place, much Italian capital had been used to improve the land on the banana plantations, and unless banana exports were resumed the capital so invested would have had to be written off as a total loss. To be sure, the Somali banana industry could not function under competitive conditions, but there appeared to be no alternative use to which the land could be put that would justify the additional investments required for continued operation of the plantations. Secondly, the Italian Government felt it had to reconcile the allegedly conflicting interests of banana producers in Somalia and citrus growers at home. Thirdly, it was clear to the Italian Government from the very beginning that trusteeship administration in Somalia would require large annual subsidies, and in this connection it seemed politically convenient to use AMB for fiscal purposes, even though it had never been so used before.[25] Only AMB, or a similar institution, could assure the smooth co-ordination of so many different, and to some extent conflicting, tasks.

In view of the above, it is not difficult to see why the banana industry in Somalia finds itself today in a precarious position. AMB keeps the industry alive through the protection it accords, but at the same time it inhibits the industry's growth. For the chief weakness of the industry lies in Italian demand, upon which AMB exerts a decisively negative influence. The fact that the industry has not been able to achieve a competitive stand-

[24] The change in name was due to the establishment of a republican régime in Italy.
[25] The fiscal question and its relation to the banana industry is of the utmost significance, but it need only be mentioned here, since it is discussed at length within the context of Somalia's budgetary and balance of payments problems in Chapter VIII.

ing after many years of activity invites a pessimistic outlook as to its future. Nevertheless it would be rash to conclude that there is no possibility of rescuing the industry from its present uneconomic position, since this position is attributable in far greater measure to policy than to immutable environmental factors.

As previously stated, the most detrimental aspect of present policy, as far as producers in Somalia are concerned, is the monopsony power which AMB exerts over them. It may be objected, however, that the behavior of AMB does not fit the concept of monopsony, since monopsony, as it is usually defined, implies the capacity to purchase at lower prices than would be charged if more than one buyer were present in the market. The statement that AMB exerts monopsony power over Somali producers, therefore, requires clarification.

In the first place, the statement refers to the effect on sellers, while the effect on the buyer is disregarded. AMB, as has been explained, does not act on behalf of consumers, and its policy is not intended to benefit them. Furthermore, AMB is a public body, and the ends for which monopsony power may be used by a public body need not always be those which are appropriate to a private firm or household.

Secondly, the statement does not apply to all sellers. It is obvious that AMB cannot exert monopsony power on the world market, since banana producers other than those in Somalia have access to alternative outlets for their produce.

Thirdly, it is true that the effect of monopsony power, in the conventional sense of the term, is to force suppliers to sell at lower prices than they might be able to obtain under different market conditions. The significance of this point, however, as far as sellers are concerned, is that their total revenues will be smaller. Now, the monopsony power which AMB exerts over Somali producers takes the form of quantitative restrictions. As for the price, since the total quantity demanded is fixed, it is determined by supply conditions. That is to say, the price which AMB pays is the same as that which any one else, including a conventional monopsony, would have to pay.[26] For at a lower price, the supply would not be forthcoming at all. Were it not for the power which AMB exerts by virtue of its position as Italy's sole importer of bananas and through its control of transportation, Somali producers would be able to sell larger quantities at lower prices, and their total revenues would in all probability increase.[27] Thus the effect on total revenues of sellers is the same in this case as under conditions of conventional monopsony.

THE PRODUCTION OF COTTON UNDER UNSTABLE CONDITIONS

COTTON CULTIVATION is for the most part concentrated in irrigated areas, although small amounts of short-staple varieties of Ugandan and American origin are grown, mostly on an experimental basis, on rain-fed lands. Where irrigation is possible several varieties of long-staple cotton of Egyptian origin can be grown, the favored variety in Somalia being *Sakellaridis*. As an exportable crop, cotton is less important than bananas. Climate and soil conditions are generally suited to its cultivation, but various technical and economic factors tend to keep its output low and variable.

The major technical difficulty is control of pests and parasites, which every year cause immense damage, thus lowering the yield of cotton per unit of land.[28] Another important factor is

[26] Assuming, of course, no miscalculations.

[27] There need be no doubt that producers in Somalia resent AMB's quantitative restrictions. In a memorandum submitted to the authorities in Italy, the producers' associations made it plain that they would welcome the abolition of AMB, provided, of course, that they could be assured of some form of protection during the time needed to adjust the industry to free market conditions. *Promemoria per S. E. Beniamino Leoni*, Rome, 1955.

[28] F. Bigi, "Recenti Sviluppi e Prospettive della Cotonicoltura in So-

labor scarcity. Cotton is a crop which must be tended by a sizable labor force, especially at the time of picking. For once the crop has matured, the lint must be gathered quickly to prevent damage from wind, rain, or other weather action. But in Somalia, because of the scarcity of labor, cotton-picking may take a month or even longer.[29]

The scarcity of labor also accounts for the fact that only a small part of the annual crop is grown directly on the plantations. Most of it is grown by Somali farmers under a contractual arrangement known as "co-participation," whereby Italian concessionaires acquire sole purchasing rights to the crop in return for the provision of seed and various facilities, as well as cash advances.[30] Co-participation thus links the production of cotton to the plantation system.

In view of the difficulties created by the scarcity of labor, some thought has been given to the advisability of using capital-intensive methods of production. There are three major obstacles, however, to the substitution of capital for labor: (1) no satisfactory way has yet been found of using machines for picking long-staple cotton; (2) the economic use of machines requires a larger scale of production than that which is practicable under Somali conditions; (3) machines are expensive.[31] In other words, the fact that labor is scarce in relation to the technical requirements for optimum output does not necessarily mean that it is also scarce in relation to capital.

Another discouraging factor is the instability of world market prices, which gives rise to violent fluctuations in the volume of cotton exports (Chart 1). As already noted, cotton was the prin-

malia," *Rivista di Agricoltura Subtropicale e Tropicale,* XLVII (1953), pp. 298–99.

[29] M. S. El Marashly, Address Delivered Before the *Istituto Culturale e Sociale* of Mogadiscio, 1955 (mimeographed).

[30] U.N. Doc. ST/TAA/J/Somaliland/R.1, p. 177.

[31] Bigi, *op. cit.,* pp. 312–15.

CHART 1

FLUCTUATIONS IN SOMALIA'S COTTON EXPORTS

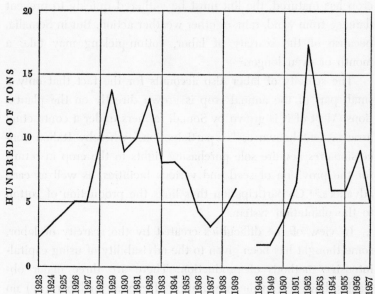

Sources: For 1923–1927, C. Noli, "L'Esportazione dei Prodotti Rurali dell'Africa Orientale Italiana dal 1921 ad Oggi," *Atti del Secondo Congresso di Studi Coloniali*, VI, Florence, 1936; for 1928–1939, U.N. Doc. T/1296; for 1948–1957, Annual Reports of the Italian Government to the United Nations on Somalia.

cipal export crop grown on the plantations in the twenties; the increasing preference which has been given to bananas since then can be attributed in large part to the instability of cotton prices on the world market.

THE PRODUCTION OF SUGAR FOR DOMESTIC CONSUMPTION

IN CONTRAST to the production of bananas, which is carried on by a large number of concessionaires grouped into three associations, the production of sugar is in the hands of a single firm, *Società Agricola Italo-Somala* (SAIS), an Italian corporation with headquarters in Genoa. Located near the middle course of the Uebi Scebeli, the SAIS estate covers an area of about 60,000 acres. About 15,000 acres are under irrigation, though no more than 10,000 are under irrigation at any one time. Nearly 5,000 acres are usually under sugar cane; the remainder is devoted to cotton, peanuts, and several other crops. SAIS also maintains a stock-breeding and dairy center. In addition, the estate is equipped with various facilities for the processing of agricultural products, such as a sugar refinery, an oil-seed pressing plant, a soap factory, and a distillery, which are connected with the irrigated farms by about 40 miles of narrow-gauge railroad track.

The production of sugar was undertaken on an experimental scale in 1921, one year after SAIS was organized.[32] Since then scientific management and the vast amount of capital at the corporation's disposal have made it possible to expand output considerably, particularly in postwar years, despite many technical difficulties as well as an inadequate and erratic labor supply.

SAIS demand for labor is essentially seasonal and tends to vary directly with rainfall, as labor is needed primarily for cutting the sugar cane.[33] The only labor available for this purpose is that represented by native farmers in nearby areas. Unlike the demand for it, however, the supply from this source tends to vary inversely with rainfall, since most natives seek employment at the plantation only when drought threatens them with famine and return to their land as soon as the weather permits resumption of subsistence farming.

Though it is not easily computed, the average wage paid by SAIS for agricultural labor appears to be low. Wages are paid

[32] R. Meregazzi, "Nuove Iniziative Agricolo-Industriali in Somalia," *Economia Nazionale*, XX, N.S., No. 1 (1928), pp. 23–26.

[33] Unless otherwise noted, the discussion of labor problems in connection with sugar production is based on data gathered by the writer at the SAIS estate in Somalia.

partly in money and partly in kind. Payments in kind consist of food, which is furnished at reduced prices, and of various facilities, such as housing and medical services, which are furnished free. Cash wages are paid on the basis of units of work accomplished, an incentive bonus being added for the completion of a certain number of units. The amount of cash an agricultural worker can earn in a day ranges between the equivalents of 20 to 40 American cents.[34] Substantially higher wages are paid for semiskilled labor, which is needed for industrial and mechanical work. SAIS—and this is worth noting—experiences no difficulty in filling the demand for this type of labor.

Fluctuations in the supply of agricultural labor have induced SAIS to use machines for cutting the sugar cane. However, manual labor is preferred and used whenever available in sufficient quantity.

It is widely believed in Somalia that SAIS difficulties with agricultural labor are chiefly the result of traditional attitudes toward work. The Somali, it is said, regards wage labor as a form of slavery; he will not, therefore, consent to work for wages except in case of dire distress. That an influence is exerted on the supply of labor by such noneconomic factors is conceivable, even probable, though the fact that SAIS encounters no problems with semiskilled labor suggests that it is not decisive. In any event it is possible to give an adequate explanation of fluctuations in the supply of agricultural labor at SAIS on the basis of economic considerations alone.

In the following illustrative diagram, the curve DD represents the demand for manual labor and the curve SS represents the supply available to SAIS during dry seasons. The quantity of labor obtained is OC and the wage is OE, the wage being determined under monopsony conditions since SAIS is the only employer of labor in the area. When a change in the weather

[34] U.N. Doc. T/1033, p. 23.

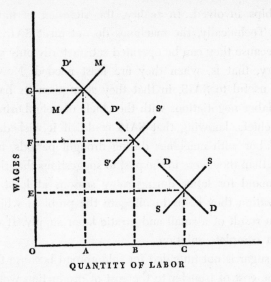

permits resumption of cultivation on subsistence farms, the supply curve of manual labor shifts to S'S'. The shift is due to the fact that the income to be earned through subsistence farming acts as a reservation price for the supply of labor at the plantation. With demand unchanged, SAIS would be able to hire the quantity OB only at the higher wage OF. But there is no demand for manual labor under these circumstances because the higher wage would unduly raise production costs and lower costs can be achieved through mechanical cutting of sugar cane. There is now, therefore, a demand for semiskilled labor to operate mechanical equipment, shown in the diagram as D'D', which is met by supply MM. The quantity of semiskilled labor obtained is OA at wage OG. Mechanical methods of cutting cane are dropped in favor of manual methods as soon as the supply curve of unskilled labor shifts back to SS, since under these conditions manual methods are cheaper.

The diagram, of course, gives an oversimplified picture of the labor situation at SAIS and is only intended to show the basic relationships involved. In reality, the situation is more complicated. Technically, the machines do not meet SAIS requirements, because they can be operated satisfactorily only when the soil is dry, that is, when they are least needed. Nevertheless they are useful to SAIS, in that they strengthen its bargaining hand in labor negotiations with the chiefs of neighboring tribes. For the chiefs, knowing that SAIS could, if it wished, replace manual labor with machines during drought periods, are more receptive than they were in the past to suggestions that they meet SAIS demand for labor during rainy seasons at least in part. Mechanization thus helps to mitigate the problem which SAIS faces as a result of a small and erratic labor supply. It does not provide a complete solution.

SAIS sugar is not intended for sale abroad because the addition of the cost of transfer to the cost of production would raise its price above that prevailing on the world market. Almost all of it is sold on the domestic market, and even then it requires some protection against foreign competition. Protection is afforded through a sliding-scale tariff which equalizes the prices of imported and SAIS sugar. In the last few years, as shown in Chart 2, protection has enabled SAIS to step up output considerably at the expense of imported sugar. At the same time the gap in the prices of domestic and imported sugar has tended to narrow, partly as a result of greater SAIS efficiency and partly as a result of an increase in the c.i.f. price of imports. In 1954, for example, the ex factory price of SAIS sugar was about $180 per ton and the margin of protection required to equalize the prices of domestic and imported sugar amounted to about $70; by 1956 the ex factory price had fallen to $170 and the margin of protection needed was only $32.[35]

A generalization often made about underdeveloped econo-

---

[35] See U.N. Doc. T/1200, p. 27; U.N. Doc. T/1344, p. 56; Annual Report of the Italian Government to the United Nations on Somalia, 1956, p. 59.

CHART 2
DOMESTIC OUTPUT AND IMPORTS OF SUGAR

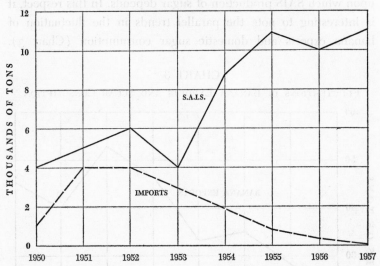

Source: Annual Reports of the Italian Government to the United Nations on Somalia.

mies is that foreign investment tends to flow toward export industries because internal markets are too small. SAIS appears to be the exception that proves the rule. In this respect, however, an important question arises as to the source of domestic purchasing power which enables SAIS to function and the means by which SAIS, a foreign corporation, is able to transfer earnings abroad. SAIS has already invested sizable amounts of foreign capital in its Somali plantation. Since 1952, for example, it has invested the equivalent of over two million dollars.[36] If it is to continue to have access to foreign capital, SAIS must be in a position to transfer interest and dividends abroad, that is, to Italy.

As for purchasing power, its obvious source is the market economy, in which the banana industry plays a dominant role. The income generated by investment in the banana industry, and

[36] U.N. Doc. T/1344, p. 56.

in activities which are connected directly or indirectly with the banana industry, provides most of the monetary buying power upon which SAIS production of sugar depends. In this respect, it is interesting to note the parallel trends in the fluctuation of banana exports and domestic sugar consumption (Chart 3).

CHART 3
FLUCTUATIONS IN BANANA EXPORTS AND SUGAR CONSUMPTION

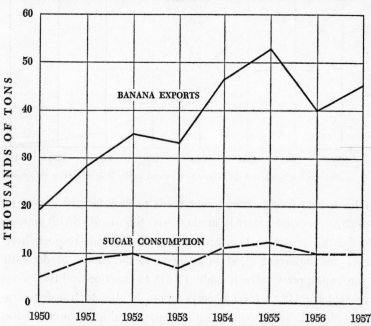

Source: Annual Reports of the Italian Government to the United Nations on Somalia.

As for the foreign exchange required to transfer SAIS earnings abroad, the two major sources are commodity exports, mainly bananas, and foreign grants. To a large extent, therefore, SAIS production of sugar depends upon the prosperity of the banana industry, a fact which underscores the strategic position which that industry occupies in the market economy of Somalia.

[CHAPTER VI]

The Structure of the Somali Economy as a Whole

——————— 🙟🙝 ———————

T HE DISCUSSION IN THE LAST THREE CHAPTERS was designed to throw into relief the major elements and characteristics of the three sectors of Somalia's economy, and for this purpose it was convenient to treat each sector as if it functioned more or less in isolation. To complete the analysis of the country's economic structure, it now becomes necessary to consider the ways in which the sectors are related to one another.

INTERSECTORAL RELATIONS

EACH SECTOR is linked with the rest of the Somali economy in two ways: through exchanges of commodities and through transfers of productive factors. It is extremely important in this case to make a sharp distinction between commodity ex-

113

changes and factor transfers because only the latter, as we shall see, affect the relative size and strength of a sector.

In general, the volume of intersectoral commodity exchanges appears to be small. Commodities are usually bartered, though there are cases where money is used as a medium of exchange. In some instances commodities are exchanged directly; in others, they are exchanged through an intermediary, the petty trader, whose role as creditor has already been discussed in connection with indigenous agriculture.

Movements of productive factors from one sector to another depend upon differences in opportunities for their employment. Differences of this kind account for fluctuations in the supply of labor on the SAIS estate; with reference to these fluctuations, we may speak, therefore, of factor transfers from indigenous agriculture to the plantation sector and vice versa. Whenever land previously used for subsistence agriculture is devoted in whole or in part to the raising of cash crops, such as cotton, for example, we may say that this involves a transfer of factors of production from indigenous agriculture to the plantation sector. Similarly, among the pastoralists who also practice farming in the rain-fed lands between the Uebi Scebeli and the Juba, more emphasis may be placed upon farming than herding or upon the latter rather than the former, depending upon conditions; such changes, from the standpoint adopted here, can be treated as transfers of factors from the pastoral sector to indigenous agriculture or vice versa. In general, as in the case of commodity flows, the quantity of factors migrating from one sector to another appears to be quite small.

These relationships, which thus far have been described in terms of a three-sector model, can also be described in terms of the more familiar two-sector model, or dual economy, in which case they may be summed up as follows: commodities and factors tend to move in small quantities within the subsistence sector (indigenous agriculture plus pastoralism) as well as between the latter and the market sector (plantation system). Commodities produced in the subsistence sector may be bartered or traded for money, but the factors used for their production have no money prices. Payment in money for the use of factors is an exclusive characteristic of the market sector. The appearance of money prices in connection with factors already devoted to some use must be taken to mean, therefore, that these factors have been transferred from the subsistence to the market sector. Through such transfers, and only through them, the market economy expands at the expense of the subsistence sector.

Thus, singular importance is attached here to the phenomenon of money prices in connection with the use of productive factors. The reason for this is that a close and necessary relation exists between such prices and a particular method of production, the so-called "roundabout" (or "indirect" or "capitalistic") method of production, which is a distinctive and vital feature of the market (or money) economy. The use of a roundabout production method means that a consumer (or final) good, instead of being turned out directly through a combination of land and labor, is produced with the aid of some other (producer or capital) good, which of course must be produced first. The process of production becomes even more roundabout when a capital good is produced with the aid of some other capital good, which, again, must be produced first. The greater the number of stages between consumer goods and the original factors required to produce them, land and labor, the more elongated is the "vertical structure of production," [1] to use G. Haberler's expression. Roundabout methods are superior to direct methods in that they make possible the production not only of a greater quantity but also of a greater variety of consumer goods, since many types of consumer goods cannot be produced at all without

[1] *Prosperity and Depression,* Cambridge, Massachusetts, 1958, p. 39.

the aid of capital goods. The strikingly higher per capita incomes which mark off developed from underdeveloped countries are due, in the main, to higher degrees of roundaboutness in the production process. These statements should not be taken to mean, however, that roundabout production is, in any sense of the word, a *cause* of economic progress. Roundabout production is superior to direct production simply because technically superior processes require its adoption in most, though not all, instances. In other words, roundabout production is a common feature of technically superior processes, but its adoption has significant economic consequences. Among other things, it introduces a large element of complexity in the organization of economic activity. Every elongation of the vertical structure of production makes the economy more productive, but it also and inevitably increases the complexity of its organization. In part this is the immediate consequence of the adoption of a more roundabout process; in part it is also the result of greater division of labor and specialization, which the increase in roundaboutness makes possible, often even necessary. It is this effect on economic organization that makes the use of money prices for factors so important. Without such prices, it would be practically impossible to calculate and compare costs in an economy based on a structure of production in which the relations of capital goods to one another, to other factors, and to other goods form a bewilderingly intricate pattern. Without such prices, therefore, a progressive economy could not function for long, if at all.

In a dual economy, then, what distinguishes the market or money sector from the subsistence sector is the payment of money for the use of productive factors. The mere use of money as a medium for the exchange of commodities shows that there is contact between the sectors, but it does not make those commodities a part of the money sector. As J. H. Boeke puts it:

The Structure of the Somali Economy as a Whole

A distinction must be made between money traffic and money economy. Money traffic means that money is used in trade by way of facilitating matters. . . . But money economy means that the whole economic system is based on money; that money, mainly productive, is employed as capital, as the foundation and point of departure for profit-making.[2]

Enough has been said to make clear that the transfer of factors, unlike that of commodities, causes the market sector to expand at the expense of the subsistence sector. In a dual economy this is the only form that development can take; for the existence of a large subsistence sector implies, as has been pointed out, that roundabout methods of production are used to a very limited degree, and so long as this condition obtains the level of income cannot be expected to rise to any appreciable extent.

In Somalia, as was stated earlier in these pages, the quantity of factors which have migrated from the subsistence sector to the market sector has been quite small thus far. It is thus obvious that expansion of the market sector is meeting with acute difficulties in this case. In the remaining sections of this chapter an attempt will be made to explain what the chief difficulties are.

THE SCARCITY OF LABOR

IN A DUAL economy the market sector serves as a link between the subsistence sector and the rest of the world. Among other things, it provides access to additional sources of technological knowledge and of capital. It thus enables the subsistence sector to develop more rapidly than under conditions of complete isolation. Though some of the capital available abroad may be obtained in the form of grants, most of it must be bor-

[2] *Economics and Economic Policy of Dual Societies as Exemplified by Indonesia*, New York, 1953, p. 67.

rowed, for capital is generally scarce. As a result development in a dual economy becomes largely dependent upon the state of foreign demand. For the necessity of paying interest and of repaying loans forces the market sector to rely on the criterion of profitability as a guide to economic activities; and the need to raise foreign exchange for the transfer of those payments abroad forces it, in addition, to concentrate upon production for export.

In Somalia there is still another factor that conditions the process of development. This is the scarcity of labor. The first Italian settlers to arrive in Somalia came, as did most of the early European settlers in Africa, in the belief that the native population would provide an abundant, and therefore cheap, source of wage labor. They reasoned that the wages which they could offer, while low by European standards, would be quite attractive to the Somalis, whose subsistence requirements were known to be minimal. They were disappointed. As time went on and as they became better acquainted with local conditions, they still found it hard to understand why their efforts to recruit a native labor force sufficiently large for their purposes should meet with so many difficulties. In the days of colonial rule the scarcity of labor formed one of the chief topics of speculative discussion among Italians concerned with Somali affairs, as the large body of Italian literature on that subject attests.

Some writers believed that the scarcity of labor was due to underpopulation.[3] It may be surmised, in view of the low density of population, that Somalia is, to some extent at least, underpopulated. Nevertheless one cannot be certain, because of a theoretical difficulty. Underpopulation may be defined as that size of population which is less than the optimum required, other

[3] T. Carletti, *I Problemi del Benadir*, Viterbo, 1912, pp. 260–61; A. Lessona, "Politica Indigena ed Economia in Somalia," *Agricoltura Coloniale*, XXIX (1935), p. 231.

factors being equal, to carry out a process of maximum development. Though the meaning of the term is clear enough, it is practically impossible to determine what the optimum would be in a concrete case, and therefore whether underpopulation (or overpopulation) obtains. But even if underpopulation does obtain in Somalia, as is probable, it cannot explain the scarcity of labor. For "underpopulation" implies that the needed manpower simply does not exist, whereas the difficulties experienced by firms in Somalia's market sector stem from their inability to induce the manpower already available in the subsistence sector to accept their offers of wage employment.

Other writers recognized this shortcoming of the underpopulation theory and concentrated instead on the shape of the supply curve of labor. As elsewhere in Africa, two opposite conclusions were reached on this subject. One group believed that the supply curve sloped upward to the right and that the scarcity of labor was due to low wages.[4] The other group claimed that the supply curve was backward-bending. The Somalis, they contended, had fixed wants; as soon as these wants were satisfied, they stopped working. To increase the supply of native labor it was therefore necessary to cut wages.[5] In the debate that ensued between these two conflicting schools of thought, the views of the second school prevailed at first. Wages were cut in 1927.[6] But the scarcity of labor continued to hinder the activities and plans of Italian entrepreneurs and managers.

Much of the fruitless speculation and confusion about the labor problem was due to the failure to realize that, since labor

[4] F. S. Caroselli, "Il Giuba e l'Avvenire della Somalia," *Rivista Coloniale,* XVI (1921), p. 173.

[5] G. Mangano, "Della Mano d'Opera nelle Nostre Colonie: Somalia Italiana," *Atti del Secondo Congresso degli Italiani all'Estero,* I, Rome, 1911; M. Rava, "Lo Sviluppo Economico della Somalia," *Rassegna Italiana,* XVI (1933), pp. 217–20.

[6] V. L. Grottanelli, "La Questione della Mano d'Opera nella Somalia Italiana," *Rivista Italiana di Scienze Economiche,* VIII, No. 9 (1936), p. 17.

must be combined with several other factors of production, it may be abundant in relation to one factor and yet scarce in relation to another. Somali labor, which at first was thought to be abundant and later was thought to be scarce, was viewed only in relation to capital. Had it really been scarce in this sense, the course to be followed would have been fairly simple. Capital being abundant, the productivity of subsistence agriculture could have been improved, within the limits of technical possibilities, by substituting capital for labor; a surplus labor force would thus have been created which could then have been siphoned off into the market sector's export industries. But capital in Somalia is actually scarce in relation to labor, while labor is scarce in relation to land. Under these circumstances an increase in the market sector's labor force will cause a decline in subsistence output and a rise in consumer imports. But imported goods compare most unfavorably, in terms of cost, with locally produced subsistence goods, owing to high costs of transportation. Wages will therefore rise steeply and, since most production in the market sector is apt to be labor-intensive (in relation to capital), so will unit costs of production, making many activities unprofitable and limiting the size of others.[7]

The fact that labor is abundant in relation to capital and at the same time scarce in relation to land favors the growth of those industries which are able to use factor proportions that most closely approximate existing scarcity ratios. It is this that gives the banana industry an edge over the production of cotton and sugar cane and that accounts, in part, for the industry's predominant role in Somalia's market sector. But this also implies a severe limitation on the number of ways in which the market sector can expand.

[7] This follows from the fact that marginal producers will be forced to drop out of the picture.

THE HIGH COST OF TRANSFER

THE HIGH COST of transportation has been mentioned as one of the chief reasons behind Somalia's labor difficulties, in view of its effect on the cost of imported goods. Its influence as a deterrent to the expansion of the money economy also makes itself felt in other ways. Among other things, as noted earlier, it raises the cost of exports and, in addition, it hinders the fusion of internal markets.

It is not difficult to account for the high cost of transportation in Somalia. Roads are few and poor; there are no railroads; and existing port facilities are not designed to handle a large volume of traffic. But attention must be called to the fact that there are other factors, less easily discerned, such as prejudices, cultural differences, lack of good will and a host of intangibles which have the same effect as inadequate means of transportation: they hamper the movement of goods from one place to another, thereby raising their cost. To describe this problem, it seems more appropriate to speak of a high cost of transfer, since cost of transfer is a more inclusive term than cost of transportation.

THE IMPORTANCE OF FOREIGN DEMAND

THE FACT that the cost of transfer is generally high does not mean, of course, that Somalia is, in an economic sense, completely isolated from the rest of the world. This much follows from the theory of comparative advantage. For according to that theory, as is well known, there are certain conditions under which it will not pay for a country to enter international trade, but these conditions are never realized in practice. What the high cost of transfer does mean is that the range of commodities entering international trade will, as a consequence, be extremely narrow. As for the terms of trade, they will, as always, be determined by reciprocal demand, though foreign demand will in this case, for obvious reasons, exert the more important influence.

Thus, once again we must emphasize the role which foreign demand plays in a dual and underdeveloped economy. Indeed this role is crucial. And it deserves all the more emphasis in view of the assumption commonly made nowadays that economic development is a primary responsibility of government. For a government is less able to influence the conditions of demand than those of supply, even when it is only a question of domestic demand; it is virtually helpless when, as in Somalia, it must reckon with foreign demand.

CHAPTER VII

The Prospects of
Development

⚭

I N THE LAST four chapters the structure of Somalia's economy was analyzed in an attempt to account for the country's poverty. It is now proposed to examine, first, the measures adopted during the trusteeship period to promote the country's economic development, and second, any alternative means and methods that might be considered in the future.

THE SEVEN YEAR PLAN

In 1952, AFIS made public the general principles which were to govern a plan for the economic development of Somalia.[1] The decision to launch such a plan, however, was not announced until two years later, when the basic features of the plan were revealed for the first time. The plan, according to of-

[1] U.N. Doc. T/1172, p. 15.

ficial statements, was scheduled for completion by the end of 1960, that is, upon termination of the trusteeship régime.

Three major influences lay behind the Italian Administration's decision. One was the pressure exerted by the United Nations Trusteeship Council, which on several occasions had urged the Italian Administration to formulate and carry out a comprehensive development plan.[2] Another was the increasingly important role of the United States International Cooperation Administration (ICA), which shortly after the establishment of the trusteeship régime had undertaken a series of technical assistance surveys and projects in Somalia. This led to frequent consultations between the Italian Administration and ICA, and American collaboration in drawing up the Seven Year Development Plan was officially acknowledged.[3] ICA, it seems, contributed heavily to the solution of technical problems involved in the execution of various projects and, in addition, played a significant part in the determination of priorities. A third factor was a study by the Italian economist G. F. Malagodi, although to what degree the study actually influenced the formulation of the Seven Year Plan is far from clear, despite official claims that the Plan followed the general lines of Malagodi's recommendations. For one thing, some of Malagodi's principal recommendations were not included in the Plan; for another, his study did not provide a suitable basis for planning, since it was essentially intended to furnish criteria that would make it possible to avoid inconsistencies in the execution of a broad but highly decentralized development policy.[4]

The Plan laid heavy emphasis upon aid to the subsistence

[2] See U.N. Doc. A/3170, p. 99, and U.N. Doc. T/1033, p. 20.

[3] W. E. Corfitzen, *Plans and Schedules for Somalia Economic Development,* USOM/Italy, 1954; U.N. Doc. T/1172, p. 16; U.N. Doc. T/1200, p. 18.

[4] See G. F. Malagodi, *Linee Programmatiche per lo Sviluppo Economico e Sociale della Somalia,* Rome, 1953; Annual Report of the Italian Government to the United Nations on Somalia, 1954, p. 65; U.N. Doc. T/1200, p. 18.

sector of the Somali economy. About 60 per cent of the total contemplated expenditure was assigned to projects designed to benefit the pastoral economy and indigenous agriculture. The remainder was allocated to communications, except for small sums which were set aside for the promotion of urban development, handicrafts, industry, and commerce.

Aid to the pastoral economy as envisaged in the Plan consisted chiefly of such projects as the excavation of shallow wells, the drilling of deep wells, and the construction of water catchment basins and other means intended to increase the supply of watering facilities for livestock. Since water development was also important for indigenous agriculture, substantial sums were allocated within the Plan for the construction of various irrigation works that would permit a more efficient utilization of flood and excess river waters. Other important projects included in the Plan for the benefit of indigenous agriculture called for clearing of additional land, construction of modern storage facilities for grain, and provision of agricultural machinery. In addition, the Plan contemplated the establishment of a special bank, the Somali Credit Institute (*Credito Somalo*), from which native farmers might obtain credit at low interest rates.

Of the total estimated expenditures for communications, nearly 80 per cent was allocated for the improvement of roads and ports. Decisions concerning this part of the Plan were preceded by intensive technical studies which resulted in the blueprinting of two alternative programs, one known as the "minimum" and the other as the "maximum" program. The former differed from the latter in that it aimed at providing transportation services for existing, as opposed to potential, centers of population and production. Thus, under the minimum program no additions were to be made to the existing road system, the only works contemplated being the paving of some roads and the stabilization, by the simple addition of sand and gravel, of others. Similarly, the port program did not call for anything beyond dredging and repairs of existing facilities at Mogadiscio, Merca, and Chisimaio. All that the minimum program aimed to accomplish was to prevent impairment of existing connections between the capital on the one hand and the Kenyan and Ethiopian borders on the other, as well as between the plantations and the sea. Under these circumstances the cost of transportation would still be high. In the absence of deep-water berths, ships arriving at Somali ports would still have to anchor in the open roadstead, a procedure requiring the use of barges and lighters for handling cargo and passengers. The maximum program, on the other hand, would have made possible some reduction in transportation costs, but the outlays required to carry it out appeared to be heavy. It was estimated, for example, that execution of the maximum port program, which only called for the modernization of facilities at two ports (Mogadiscio and Merca), would cost about one hundred times as much as what was envisaged under the minimum program. Because of the huge outlays required by the maximum program, as well as for other reasons, AFIS deemed it advisable to limit its efforts to the execution of the minimum program, and ICA concurred in this view.[5]

It was originally estimated that fulfillment of the Seven Year Plan would cost the equivalent of approximately ten million dollars. This figure excludes investment on private account, although official statements include estimates of the private investment expected to follow as a direct and immediate consequence of the execution of public investment projects.[6] Inasmuch as decisions concerning private investment are not subject to the control of

[5] See A. J. Van Dyke, *Road Study in Somalia, East Africa,* USOM/Italy, 1953; F. G. Reinicke, *Port Survey in Somalia, East Africa,* USOM/Italy, 1954.

[6] AFIS, *Plans de Développement Economique de la Somalie, Années 1954–1960,* Rome, 1954.

the planning authorities, it does not seem appropriate to treat such investment as an integral part of the Seven Year Plan.

In 1955, estimates for investment in agriculture were revised upward, and a year later the whole Plan was revised in the same direction. The increase in estimated expenditures was due for the most part to the addition of a number of projects and could not be attributed, save for a negligible proportion, to cost inflation. While total estimated expenditures thus increased, the relative shares of different investment categories remained roughly the same (Table 18). The change brought about by the revision of estimated expenditures was therefore solely one of magnitude; it did not affect either the character or the orientation of the Plan.

TABLE 18

ESTIMATED EXPENDITURES UNDER THE SEVEN YEAR
DEVELOPMENT PLAN

| INVESTMENT CATEGORY | ORIGINAL PLAN | | REVISED PLAN | | |
	Thousands of U.S. $ Equivalents	Per Cent of Total	Thousands of U.S. $ Equivalents	Per Cent of Total	Percentage Change
Livestock	2,376	24.0	3,370	24.7	+41.4
Agriculture	3,506	35.2	5,097	37.4	+45.3
Communications	3,360	33.8	4,281	31.4	+27.4
Urban development, handicrafts, industry, commerce	696	7.0	871	6.5	+25.1
Total	9,938	100.0	13,619	100.0	+37.0

Sources: AFIS, *Plans de Développement Economique de la Somalie, Années 1954–1960*, Rome, 1954; Annual Report of the Italian Government to the United Nations on Somalia, 1956. Figures for agriculture include the initial capital of the Somali Credit Institute.

In its original form the Plan contained, in addition to an estimate of global expenditures, a list of the expenditure targets to be aimed at during the first year of operation. These targets were not reached (Table 19). In view of the revisions which subsequently took place, however, the results of the first year are not necessarily indicative of the rate of plan fulfillment in later periods. In any event, no detailed statements or estimates were

TABLE 19

ESTIMATED AND ACTUAL EXPENDITURES FOR 1954
UNDER THE ORIGINAL DEVELOPMENT PLAN

INVESTMENT CATEGORY	EXPENDITURES (Thousands of U.S. $ Equivalents)		NONFULFILLMENT (%)
	Estimated	Actual	
Livestock	745	271	63.7
Agriculture	976	836	14.4
Communications	827	542	34.5
Urban development, handicrafts, industry, commerce	97	34	65.0
Total	2,645	1,683	36.4

Sources: AFIS, *Plans de Développement Economique de la Somalie, Années 1954–1960,* Rome, 1954; Annual Report of the Italian Government to the United Nations on Somalia, 1955. Figures for livestock and agriculture do not include disbursements by the Somalia Development Fund and ICA contributions.

published concerning annual targets to be reached in 1955 and thereafter. The United Nations mission that visited Somalia in 1954 reported that annual expenditures were apparently expected to be equal to the annual average of total estimated expenditures, but that physical planning, in the sense of decisions concerning specific projects to be set up, was to be confined to the year immediately ahead.[7] A comparison of actual expenditures with yearly averages of total estimated outlays leads to the conclusion that the execution of the Plan was ahead of schedule by the end

[7] U.N. Doc. T/1200, p. 20. See also Annual Report of the Italian Government to the United Nations on Somalia, 1957, p. 62.

TABLE 20

CUMULATIVE TOTALS OF ANNUAL EXPENDITURES IN 1954–1957, AS
PERCENTAGES OF ESTIMATED TOTAL EXPENDITURES REQUIRED
FOR COMPLETION OF THE REVISED DEVELOPMENT PLAN

INVESTMENT CATEGORY	1954	1955	1956	1957
Livestock	17.4	32.0	43.5	66.2
Agriculture	16.4	37.6	57.8	67.1
Communications	12.6	36.6	49.6	60.3
Urban development, handicrafts, industry, commerce	3.8	11.7	35.2	62.4
Total, all categories	**14.6**	**34.3**	**50.2**	**64.4**

Source: Annual Reports of the Italian Government to the United Nations on Somalia.

of the first four years (Table 20). As a technique for measuring
the rate of plan fulfillment, however, comparisons of this kind
are misleading, since physical planning is bound to affect estimates of annual outlays. Moreover, the estimates for the first year
clearly indicate that annual expenditures were not expected to
coincide with yearly averages. It can only be inferred that what
in reality occurred was that, after the first year's experience, the
planners thought it best to adopt a flexible procedure in regard
to implementation of the Plan and consequently were unable to
forecast results on a year-to-year basis.

The planners' desire for flexibility can be attributed in large
part to uncertainties regarding sources of finance. Chronic deficits
in the Administration's budget (which are discussed in the next
chapter) precluded the use of domestic revenues for financing
the Plan, while the character of the projects ruled out any recourse to loan capital, whether domestic or foreign; exclusive
reliance had therefore to be placed upon grants, of which there
were only three likely sources: private contributions, United
States Government grants-in-aid, and Italian Government subsidies.

TABLE 21

SOURCES OF FINANCE FOR THE DEVELOPMENT PLAN

SOURCE	THOUSANDS OF U.S. $ EQUIVALENTS	Per Cent of Revised Plan
Private grants	318	2.3
SACA	(133)	
SAG	(119)	
SAIS	(66)	
U.S. grants	2,209	16.2
USOM operations	(317)	
Contributions to Somalia Development Fund	(1,892)	
Italian grants	7,561	55.5
Expenditures and commitments as of December 31, 1957	(6,469)	
Contributions to Somalia Development Fund	(1,092)	
Total, all sources	10,088	74.0

Sources: U.N. Doc. T/1372; Annual Reports of the Italian Government to the United Nations on Somalia. The figures cited in the table are based on information available in 1958. An attempt to check the statistics on U.S. grants with those quoted by ICA in Washington, D.C., showed substantial agreement; it was not possible, however, to verify them in detail, because of differences in the accounting procedures used by AFIS and ICA.

Little more than 2 per cent of total requirements was obtained from private sources (Table 21). SAIS and SAG pledged some funds for road improvement, and SACA made available a small sum for aid to the pastoral economy and, jointly with SAG, contributed to the initial capital of the Somali Credit Institute.[8]

More substantial sums were made available by the United States Government under its foreign aid program. In the early years of the trusteeship régime, the United States inaugurated a well-drilling project which later came to be regarded as an integral part of the revised Development Plan. Moreover in June,

[8] Private grants should not be confused with investment on private account, since they are used for public investment purposes and are "private" only with respect to source.

1954, the United States and Italy signed an agreement whereby a Somalia Development Fund was created. After an initial contribution, the United States added to the Fund's resources in 1957 and again in 1958. Italy matched the first two amounts remitted by the United States, but thereafter, it seems, made available a sum equal to only one-fifth of the latest American contribution.[9] The Fund's financial resources were used to carry out some of the projects within the Plan, but their disbursement was placed under joint Italian-American control. Thus the United States acquired some responsibility for implementation of the Plan.[10]

The balance of the funds used for financing the Plan came from subsidies which the Italian Government normally accorded to AFIS every year in anticipation of deficits in Somalia's budget, and it is in this connection that there arose an element of uncertainty. For the capital to be obtained through this source for development purposes represented residual funds, the amount of which could vary depending upon two factors: the size of the annual subsidy, which in turn depended upon decisions taken in Rome, and the size of the deficit in Somalia's ordinary budget. This made it difficult for the planners to calculate far in advance how much finance would actually be available for development in any one particular year.

EVALUATION OF THE PLAN

FROM THE standpoint of economic analysis, the Seven Year Plan raises two basic questions. One is what is meant by

[9] Annual Report of the Italian Government to the United Nations on Somalia, 1957, p. 55; U.N. Doc. T/1372, Annex VI, pp. 4–5.

[10] Financing of the well-drilling project and contributions to the Somalia Development Fund do not represent the full measure of American economic aid to Somalia. Additional funds were used for technical assistance. These are not shown in Table 21 because technical assistance is not included in the Plan.

"planning" in this context, and the other is whether it is actually designed to promote the economic development of the country, and if so, to what extent.

With regard to the first question, it must be emphasized from the very outset that the Seven Year Plan is not a central plan. The planners in Somalia do not control all sources of investment expenditure in the country. As Table 22 shows, private investment is, on the average, nearly twice as large as public investment. It should be noted, however, that about 75 per cent of all private investment is accounted for by prospecting for oil; if

TABLE 22

PUBLIC AND PRIVATE INVESTMENT IN SOMALIA, 1954–1957
(*Millions of U.S. $ Equivalents*)

ITEM	1954	1955	1956	1957	1954–1957
Public investment					
Expenditures under the Development Plan	2.0	2.7	2.2	1.9	8.8
Other public investment, excluding normal maintenance of public facilities	1.3	1.3	0.9	0.5	4.0
Total	3.3	4.0	3.1	2.4	12.8
Private investment					
Oil prospecting	1.6	3.0	5.6	5.6	15.8
Other private investment	1.3	1.3	1.3	1.9	5.8
Total	2.9	4.3	6.9	7.5	21.6
Total public and private investment	6.2	8.3	10.0	9.9	34.4

Source: U.N. Doc. T/1372.

this item is excluded, private investment amounts to only one-half of public investment.

Furthermore, the Plan is relatively limited in scope, since on the average it accounts for only about two-thirds of total public investment (Table 22). It does not include, for example, expenditures on public health or education, although social services are generally recognized as having an important bearing on economic development. The plan, therefore, does not meet the United Nations Trusteeship Council's expressed desire for a comprehensive development program, a result which is hardly surprising in view of the lack of basic statistics and of the uncertainties concerning finance. For under these conditions a certain amount of flexibility and decentralization in the investment decision-making process is practically inevitable, and it is hard to reconcile flexibility and decentralization with the concept of economic planning.

It has been suggested that the Seven Year Plan, despite its name, is in reality a public works program.[11] Strictly speaking, this is not an accurate view. Some of the projects within the Plan, such as, for example, the provision of agricultural credit, are not classifiable as public works in the ordinary sense of the term. Moreover, a number of public works projects are financed and carried out outside the Plan. Actually, the term "plan" here seems to mean nothing more than a public statement of the authorities' intention to complete a series of long-term public investment projects (described only in general terms) within a specified number of years, provided that financial and other obstacles can be overcome.

Even more important than the meaning of planning is the question of the extent of economic development that the Plan can be expected to promote. For an answer to this question we must look at the allocation of capital resources and at the character of the projects within the Plan.

As Table 18 shows, the Plan allocates a sum for the development of livestock and agriculture that is twice as large as that allocated for the improvement of communications. Since in this case agriculture does not include the banana and sugar plantations, development of livestock and agriculture is more or less synonymous with economic aid to the subsistence sector, whereas improvement of transportation is of course an activity closely con-

[11] U.N. Doc. T/1172, p. 16.

nected with the market sector. Hence, if minor items are excluded, it may be said that capital resources within the Plan have been allocated to the subsistence and market sectors of the economy in a ratio of approximately two to one.

In principle, economic aid to a subsistence sector may differ in form as well as in substance, depending upon the aims one seeks to fulfill. It may be so designed as to induce a permanent transfer of productive factors to the market sector; or it may be merely intended to strengthen subsistence activities and thus leave the economic structure of the country more or less unchanged. The character of the projects within the Seven Year Plan leaves little room for doubt as to the alternative chosen by the planners in Somalia. New wells, irrigation works, silos, agricultural machinery, and all the other facilities to be provided had only one purpose: to decrease economic insecurity in the subsistence sector. For the additional output which these projects would make possible could not be linked with market demand without a significant reduction in the cost of transfer; and the fact that the minimum transportation program was adopted in preference to the maximum program shows that a reduction in the cost of transfer was not one of the planners' aims.

The conclusion that the Plan was primarily intended to strengthen the subsistence sector rather than to enlarge the market economy is further supported by an examination of the criteria that guided the allocation of capital resources. An important criterion was supplied by ICA. The American agency insisted that in order to help Somalia achieve political independence within the short period of ten years, funds should be used for the benefit of the "indigenous" rather than of the "European" economy, even though such a policy would mean slow economic progress. ICA recognized that development of transportation would benefit the whole economy in the long run, but since only Europeans were likely to gain in the short run, it felt that no substantial funds should be devoted to this purpose.[12] These views were expressed with reference to ICA funds only, but in the light of the important role assumed by ICA in the formulation as well as in the execution of the Plan, they were bound to influence thinking about the disposition of other capital resources as well.

The criterion formulated by ICA strongly suggests that economic development was not the primary objective of the Seven Year Plan. From an economic standpoint, the ethnic distinctions that it invokes are largely irrelevant, and the reasoning on which it is based is inconsistent with the assumption that development is the Plan's basic objective. For if such an assumption is made, the logical course of action appears to be precisely the opposite of the one advocated by ICA; that is, funds should be devoted primarily to projects likely to benefit the whole economy in the long run, even if some special groups or interests might thereby reap most of the immediate advantages.

Another important factor was the Italian Administration's concern, in view of the uncertainties about finance, over the high cost of the maximum program for roads and ports. This apparently resulted in the placing of emphasis on relatively low-cost projects. Closely related to this was the planners' adherence to the principle that the extent of transportation facilities must be justified by the volume of output. It was on the basis of these considerations that the minimum program was chosen in preference to the maximum program. Though it may be agreed that transportation must be justified by production, it can also be argued that production must be justified by transportation. Many historical examples support the thesis that development of transportation may precede that of production. An almost classic example is the Kenya-Uganda Railway, the construction of which preceded and indeed made possible the development of cotton production in Uganda.

[12] Corfitzen, *op. cit.*, p. 24.

In other words, the relation between transportation and production can be expressed as a function, but whether transportation or production should be regarded as the independent variable is largely a matter of taste. The choice made in Somalia can therefore be explained only as the result of caution and conservatism on the part of the planners.

These critical comments are not meant to belittle or disparage the efforts of AFIS and ICA to promote the welfare of the people of Somalia. The formulation as well as the execution of the Seven Year Plan required consideration of many other problems besides economic ones. There were, for instance, complex technical questions which had to be solved, and the layman who has had a chance to observe the course of events during the trusteeship period cannot but feel that the collaboration between AFIS and ICA furnishes an outstanding illustration of technical cooperation and achievement in what is, after all, a difficult and often trying physical as well as human environment. Economic analysis alone provides too narrow a basis for the expression of a balanced judgment about an undertaking as complex as the Seven Year Plan. Such critical remarks as have been made were intended to serve only one purpose: to make clear that the Plan was not, as a matter of fact, designed to achieve economic development. For the actual objectives were different and essentially noneconomic. Thus, for example, the water development program was in fact designed to induce the herder to adopt a sedentary way of life, so as to ease the task of giving him a modern education. For it is difficult to bring modern education to a nomad; because of this, and partly also as a consequence of nomadism itself, the nomadic herder's participation in the democratic processes of the new state of Somalia is not likely to be very effective. Similarly, the various projects set up for the benefit of indigenous agriculture were aimed at decreasing economic insecurity, in the hope that Somalia would thus be helped, if only in a small measure, to achieve and maintain political stability.

One may be tempted to object to the assertion that the Seven Year Plan was not designed to promote Somalia's economic growth on the ground that social services, such as education, and various other noneconomic factors usually have an important bearing on the process of development. But the statement that such factors play a useful role in connection with development is subject to certain qualifications. W. A. Lewis has pointed out that whereas certain kinds of education, such as technical training, constitute a form of social investment, other kinds, such as studies in fine arts, are merely a form of consumption.[13] Where economic development is the guiding objective, it is important to distinguish between education as social investment and education as consumption, though not necessarily along the lines drawn by Lewis; for one may share Alfred Marshall's view that anything that improves the human mind is apt to promote economic development.[14] Nevertheless it can be maintained that education, even from Marshall's standpoint, constitutes social investment only if other requirements of the development process are also being fulfilled; otherwise it is a form of consumption, for it can only be enjoyed for its own sake. And the same can be said of other noneconomic factors.

There is another important reason that the projects in the Seven Year Plan, despite their nature, tend to be associated with the idea of economic development. This is the confusion caused by the prevailing concept of investment, according to which any addition to the national stock of capital equipment is automatically considered to be investment. The modern approach thus stresses the purely quantitative aspects of investment. It neglects the fact

[13] *The Theory of Economic Growth*, Homewood, Illinois, 1955, pp. 183–84.
[14] *Principles of Economics*, London, 1920, Book II, Ch. 2 and Book IV, Ch. 6; "The Future of the Working Classes," *Memorials of Alfred Marshall*, A. C. Pigou, ed., London, 1925.

that, at bottom, investment is a process involving long-term changes in economic structure, inasmuch as there is no purpose to the creation and utilization of capital goods other than that of making possible an increase in the quantity and variety of consumer goods in the future. But capital goods, it must be remembered, wear out; investment can never succeed, therefore, unless the capital goods used in the process increase economic values to an extent and in a manner adequate to cover, at a minimum, the need for replacement. The modern quantitative approach tends to obscure this elementary, but vital, characteristic of investment. Ordinarily it gives rise to no special difficulties, because in most cases provision for replacement can be taken for granted. Thus, in the case of private investment, the desire for profit can be expected to prevent the need for replacement from being overlooked. In the case of public investment financed through loans, the obligation to pay interest and to repay the principal can be expected to have the same effect. If public investment is financed out of taxes, there is apt to be some pressure to consider the need for replacement because of the well-known reluctance of political leaders to increase taxation. And if it is paid for through deficit financing, there is likely to be much concern over the consequences of inflation. But a different situation arises when capital projects are financed out of grants; for here there is no built-in inducement to consider depreciation.

As a matter of fact, the Seven Year Plan makes no provision for wear and tear and obsolescence. The capital projects envisaged in the Plan may well increase output in the subsistence sector, but this does not mean that the increased output, given the very nature of a subsistence economy, will provide the means for replacement of capital goods. Under these conditions, to aid pastoralism and indigenous agriculture by making capital equipment available for the production of additional consumer goods is not essentially different from the outright provision of the latter. It is of course not to be denied that the capital goods made available under the Plan will benefit the Somali economy in some way; in the future they may even come to play an important role in fostering economic development, as a result of as yet unforeseeable events. But these arguments for provision of capital equipment can be used just as well to justify assistance in the form of outright provision of consumer goods.

It will perhaps be asked why the available grant capital was not utilized to carry out a development policy. The answer to this question is given by the Plan's authors themselves, who from the beginning appeared to be fully conscious of the fact that the projects they had decided to carry out did not involve structural changes in the country's economy. They point out that a development policy would have meant undertaking various projects which could not have been completed by 1960; in view of the extreme uncertainty in their minds, as well as in those of many others, about conditions in Somalia after the end of trusteeship, prudence seemed to dictate that such a policy should not be embarked upon.[15] The major difficulty was therefore the time element, and this difficulty can be traced directly to the United Nations decision to set a deadline for the independence of Somalia.

This point is particularly significant, since it illustrates the effect that a purely political decision can have on the course of economic development. As was observed in the introduction to this book, there is no evidence that the United Nations took economic consequences into account when it decided the political fate of Somalia. On the contrary, its action appeared to be guided by the view that political decisions are basically unrelated to economic development, and that the latter can in any event be so tailored as to meet the exigencies of political change. It is not always feasible to do so, however, and in this case it proved to be impossible. The explanation for this lies in the disparate na-

[15] AFIS, *Plans*, pp. 5–7.

ture of the determinants of political and economic change. Political conditions can be altered quite rapidly, since, in the final analysis, political changes depend upon an expression of the human will. But the same is not true of changes in economic structure, since, among other things, they depend upon a time-consuming investment process. How much time may be required for economic change will depend upon the specific determinants of the type of investment appropriate to a given situation, and these determinants, as is always the case with economic phenomena, will consist of elements that are partly subjective and partly objective. Development policies are therefore subject to certain rigidities and cannot be counted upon in all instances to permit a smooth adjustment to changing political conditions.

THE SOMALI CREDIT INSTITUTE

As ALREADY MENTIONED, the initial capital of the Somali Credit Institute—amounting to the equivalent of about 800,000 dollars, including contributions by SACA and SAG of nearly one-fifth of the total—was provided under the Plan. Though the Institute may be regarded, for this and other reasons, as an integral part of the Plan, its policies and operations are of sufficient importance to deserve separate discussion.

The Somali Credit Institute was established in 1954, chiefly to provide short- and medium-term credit for persons not normally eligible for loans at commercial banks. At first it was not allowed to handle deposit and savings accounts, since it was not expected to perform commercial bank functions. For it was created in the hope that, by making loans available at interest rates far below those customarily charged by petty traders, it would help to reduce indebtedness in indigenous agriculture.

One of the first problems to confront the Institute was to determine what these rates should be. It was decided that in this matter the Einaudi Law on agricultural credit in Italy should be followed. This meant that the interest rates to be charged by the Institute could not exceed the official discount rate, which was then 4 per cent. Credit thus became available to subsistence farmers at rates ranging between 4 and 5.5 per cent, depending on the duration of the loan.[16] It is necessary to point out that the Einaudi Law was passed with reference to agricultural conditions in Italy; in Somalia, where agricultural conditions are radically different, it could only serve as a convenient but arbitrary formula for the determination of interest rates.

The Institute was required to grant loans to subsistence farmers whenever such loans could be expected to contribute to an increase in output. The problem of repayment arising out of the fact that most subsistence farmers usually have no money was to be met through a government stockpiling program. Farmers would sell their crops to the government under this program and receive in payment such sums as were due to them after deduction of the principal of the loan plus interest. Because of the close connection between agricultural credit and stockpiling, management of the stockpiling program was initially entrusted to the Institute. The program was not only intended to enable the Institute to recover funds loaned to subsistence farmers; it was also designed to meet future emergencies with regard to food supplies for the native population such as might arise, for example, as a result of unfavorable seasonal factors. The basic ideas governing the program were simple. During seasons of relatively abundant harvests, the government would purchase grain at prices higher than those prevailing on the market. The grain thus purchased could be preserved for a long time, thanks to the modern storage facilities provided under the Plan. Should the country suddenly be threatened with a temporary food shortage, the gov-

[16] AFIS, *Bollettino Ufficiale*, No. 3, Supp. 1, March 2, 1954; *ibid.*, No. 8, August 2, 1954.

ernment would release grain to the public at prices below market levels and thus check speculative price rises.

The Institute was also entrusted with the administration of a special program designed to make agricultural machinery purchased under the Plan available to subsistence farmers on a rental basis. Farmers were required to pay rental fees in cash, but if unable to do so they could be extended credit. As was to be expected, most of the fees eventually collected were financed through credit: in 1956, for example, credit represented about 70 per cent of all fees collected.[17]

The Institute began to operate under highly inauspicious circumstances, as 1954 was a year marked by widespread crop failures in Somalia. To meet the emergency, grain had to be imported and sold below cost.[18] During the three years that followed, seasonal factors in agriculture were more favorable and some grain reserves were accumulated. But the Institute, as Table 23 shows, incurred huge deficits.

TABLE 23

LOSSES INCURRED BY THE SOMALI CREDIT INSTITUTE, 1954–1957
(*Thousands of U.S. $ Equivalents*)

YEAR	OUTLAYS	RECEIPTS	DEFICIT
1954	28.1	3.5	24.6
1955	69.7	14.3	55.4
1956	108.5	35.5	73.0
1957	102.5	38.7	63.8

Source: Somali Credit Institute (communication to the author). Figures for 1954 represent only six months of activity.

In 1957, the Somali Credit Institute was reorganized. A law passed at the end of 1956 authorized the Institute to provide deposit and savings account facilities. This had the effect of increasing to some extent the lending capacity of the bank. More-

[17] Credito Somalo, *Bilancio 1956*, Mogadiscio, 1957.
[18] Annual Report of the Italian Government to the United Nations on Somalia, 1954, p. 60.

over, administration of the stockpiling program and of the renting of agricultural machinery to subsistence farmers was turned over to a new public agency, *Ente Nazionale Ammassi e Motoaratura* (ENAM). This step involved no fundamental changes in the arrangements intended to serve as the basis for agricultural credit. Nevertheless it was a helpful step forward, in that it freed the Institute from responsibilities far removed from banking functions and enabled it to reduce administrative expenses. But, despite these improvements, the Institute's profit and loss account continued to show large deficits, and so did ENAM's.

The persistence of deficits is explained by the fact that the Institute was required to charge an interest rate lower than the market rate. This created an imbalance between the demand and supply of loanable funds which was reflected in a drop of the Institute's earnings below the cost of lending. Output of indigenous agriculture in 1954–1957 was fairly high on the average, but there were many individual crop failures. Since the Institute was a public body created expressly for the purpose of achieving certain social goals, it was required to extend credit in instances where no ordinary banking institution would be expected to. Consequently the volume of lending could not fall below a certain minimum, and the gap between earnings and lending costs had to be filled by Italian Administration subsidies.

In view of these deficits, it is clear that the creation of the Somali Credit Institute and of ENAM, though it has of course dealt a severe blow to the lending activities of petty traders, has not caused the burden of indebtedness on the economy as a whole to be reduced, but merely to be shifted. That is to say, the burden previously borne by indigenous agriculture is now largely shouldered by public institutions. There are those who maintain that the creation of these institutions has nonetheless resulted in a net economic gain for Somalia. They point to the fact that during 1954–1957 domestic agricultural output rose to such an extent that grain reserves could be accumulated and imports no longer had to be relied upon to stave off threats of famine within the country. But the rise in output, it should be observed, was largely due to seasonal factors; it may therefore be only a temporary phenomenon. In any event, the point here is not whether the Institute and ENAM have benefited indigenous agriculture. It may well be that they have, at least in some measure. The point is that as instruments of economic development they leave much to be desired; for they are designed to treat the symptoms and not the causes of distress in indigenous agriculture.

ALTERNATIVE APPROACHES

SINCE THE Seven Year Plan does not appear to offer any genuine hope of rapid economic development, the question arises whether any alternative solution to the problem exists. Many people, in and out of Somalia, seem to think that the discovery of oil may provide it. There is much activity, involving American, Italian and Dutch companies, in connection with the search for oil. Prospecting for oil is in fact the largest single item of investment in Somalia. On the average nearly twice as much is spent on it as on public investment within the Seven Year Plan.

The high hopes that are being entertained of the economic results of possible oil discoveries in Somalia are largely based on a misconception of the role that natural resources play in the process of economic development.[19] Oil may indeed become the basis of some development, but only if certain obstacles can be overcome. Should substantial quantities of oil be found in Somalia, the problem of high transportation costs would still have to be solved before the oil could reach a market. It may be argued that the large expenditures required for the improvement of transportation would then be justified, but some doubt can be ex-

[19] See p. 38.

pressed in this regard. Since Somalia lies in the vicinity of Near Eastern sources of oil, it is not likely to enjoy a competitive advantage vis-à-vis Arabian suppliers when it comes to distant markets, even if better transportation facilities within the country are provided. As for nearby markets, these are too small to warrant large expenditures for transportation, and without an improved transportation system Somali suppliers will almost certainly be at a disadvantage vis-à-vis their Near Eastern competitors. In Ethiopia, for example, there is only a limited demand for fuels, and Arabian oil shipped via Jibuti and the Franco-Ethiopian railway is more than likely to cost Ethiopians less than oil from Somalia.

But even if Somalia did find a way to market substantial quantities of oil, this would not necessarily lead to the economic development of the country. As pointed out by the World Bank mission to Somalia, much would depend upon how oil revenues would be utilized.[20] In other words, even under the most optimistic assumptions, the discovery of oil could lead to development only if a suitable economic policy were formulated and firmly adhered to.

Such a policy will be needed in Somalia whether oil is discovered or not. To be successful, it will have to meet several requirements. Some of these requirements can be usefully discussed only after the consideration of certain problems of public finance and international trade. These are dealt with in the next chapter. One thing, however, should be fairly clear at this point: a policy aiming at development of the country cannot succeed, given the dual character of the economy, if it does not seek to encourage the transfer of productive factors from the subsistence to the market sector.

[20] U.N. Doc. T/1296, p. 2.

CHAPTER VIII

The Problem of Financial Dependence

———— ❦ ————

I N THIS CHAPTER it is proposed to discuss the problem of financial dependence, its nature and its relation to economic development in Somalia. The problem arises as a result of annual
deficits in the public budget and in the balance of payments. At
bottom, these deficits reflect the fact that Somalia habitually en-
joys a level of income which, though it is low in comparison with
the income levels enjoyed by developed countries, is nevertheless higher than that which the social output of the country alone
can justify. Analysis of the public budget and of the balance of
payments should help to make this point clear.

THE PUBLIC BUDGET

As TABLE 24 shows, annual deficits in the over-all
public budget during the trusteeship period amounted on the

average to the equivalent of about eight million dollars, representing nearly 60 per cent of total expenditures. Deficits in the ordinary budget averaged only slightly less, about seven and a half million dollars, or 55 per cent of ordinary expenditures. All these deficits were met out of Italian Government grants.

TABLE 24

GOVERNMENT EXPENDITURES AND REVENUES IN SOMALIA
(Millions of U.S. $ Equivalents)

ITEM	1951	1952	1953	1954	1955	1956	1957
EXPENDITURES							
General administration	5.1	5.7	5.9	5.8	2.5	2.7	2.9
Economic services	1.0	0.9	0.8	0.8	1.6	1.9	2.0
Social services	0.9	0.9	1.1	1.1	2.6	2.9	2.7
Security	9.5	5.0	4.0	3.3	5.0	5.0	4.3
Miscellaneous	0.4	0.4	0.2	0.4	0.8	0.7	0.7
Total ordinary expenditures	16.9	12.9	12.0	11.4	12.5	13.2	12.6
Extraordinary expenditures	1.4	1.3	0.8	0.9	1.5	1.7	1.5
Total	18.3	14.2	12.8	12.3	14.0	14.9	14.1
REVENUES							
Income taxes	0.2	0.3	0.3	0.6	0.4	0.6	0.7
Property taxes	n	n	n	n	0.1	0.1	n
Commodity taxes	2.5	2.5	2.1	2.3	3.1	3.2	3.9
Government fees and commercial revenues	1.9	1.9	1.7	1.8	1.9	2.0	2.2
Miscellaneous	0.2	0.1	0.2	0.5	0.3	0.3	0.1
Total ordinary revenues	4.8	4.8	4.3	5.2	5.8	6.2	6.9
Italian Government subsidies	13.5	9.4	8.5	7.1	8.2	8.7	7.2
Total	18.3	14.2	12.8	12.3	14.0	14.9	14.1

Source: Government of Somalia, Ministry for Financial Affairs (communication to the author).
n = negligible.

It may be noticed that total ordinary expenditures and those required for the maintenance of security have tended to remain fairly stable since 1952 (Table 24). Expenditures for general administration have declined since 1954, but the decline has been accompanied by a rise in expenditures for economic and social services. To a large extent these changes reflect changes in the formal organization of government administration rather than in the nature of expenditures incurred, since many items originally included in "general administration" were later reclassified as economic and social services.

It may also be noticed that if expenditures were reduced to the level of revenues, little or nothing would be left over to provide for other government services after meeting the needs, at present levels, of defense, internal security, and administration of justice. In a country of the size and population of Somalia, current expenditures for security—which run somewhere between four and five million dollars annually—must be judged to be at or near the minimum required for the protection of life and property; a drastic slash in these expenditures, while it might make some room for the provision of other government services, would not therefore be practical. It is thus clear that the deficit in the public budget cannot be wiped out merely by reducing expenditures; for if this were done, the most essential government services could no longer be assured.

As is characteristic of most underdeveloped countries, indirect taxation provides the largest source of government revenues in Somalia. Taxes on commodities—mainly duties on imports and exports and levies on sugar consumption—account for about one-half of all revenues. An attempt has been made to increase the taxation of property through the imposition of a special tax on native holdings of agricultural land (the so-called "shamba tax"), but the yield has been negligible and collection has been hampered by popular hostility.[1] In view of the country's extremely low level of income, the possibility of eliminating or even of substantially reducing the deficit in the public budget by means of additional taxation, direct or indirect, cannot be entertained with any degree of confidence.

A tentative estimate by AFIS indicates that the annual deficit in the public budget during the first two years of independence

[1] See U.N. Doc. T/1344, pp. 41–42.

may be of the order of five million dollars, or three million less than the average for 1952–1957. The estimate was made on the assumption that revenues would increase somewhat, while expenditures—including those for the services of foreign technicians and advisers, as well as some outlays for economic development —would remain more or less constant.[2] AFIS views on future revenues may be a little too optimistic, but even if these are taken for granted it is patent that neither a reduction in expenditures nor an increase in revenues, nor a combination of the two, can provide a practical means of wiping out chronic deficits in the public budget.

THE BALANCE OF PAYMENTS

THE BALANCE of payments of Somalia shows an annual deficit which, on the average, amounts to the equivalent of about nine and a half million dollars. Thus far the country has been spared a general shortage of foreign exchange, owing to the willingness of the Italian Government to make grant funds available. Both the balance of trade and the balance of invisibles show chronic deficits. Those in the balance of invisibles are usually larger, mainly on account of remittances abroad by foreign officials and technical personnel (Table 25). In the opinion of the World Bank Mission to Somalia, there is also reason to believe that some capital revenue, in addition to the amounts shown in Table 25, is flowing out of the country in the guise of personal remittances.[3]

As for the balance of trade, it has been passive ever since 1897, when Italy first assumed responsibility for the administration of Somalia (Table 26). Balance of payments statistics are

[2] AFIS, *Economic Requirements of the Territory of Somalia on the Expiration of the Trusteeship Mandate*, Rome, 1958.
[3] U.N. Doc. T/1296, p. 67.

TABLE 25

The Balance of Payments of Somalia

(*Millions of U.S. $ Equivalents*)

Item	1951	1952	1953	1954	1955	1956	1957
Commodity trade	−5.3	−3.6	−2.3	−1.8	−2.4	−3.8	−2.9
Invisibles	−4.9	−7.1	−8.8	−5.8	−6.6	−6.7	−4.4
Transport	(−0.4)	(−1.0)	(−1.2)	(−0.8)	(−1.8)	(−1.0)	(−0.9)
Travel	(−0.1)	(−0.7)	(−0.4)	(−0.3)	(−0.2)	(−0.1)	(−0.1)
Personal remittances	(−3.6)	(−4.8)	(−7.0)	(−4.4)	(−3.7)	(−4.4)	(−2.5)
Capital revenue	(−0.1)	(−0.6)	(−0.4)	(−0.5)	(−1.2)	(−1.6)	(−1.0)
Other	(−0.7)	(—)	(+0.2)	(+0.2)	(+0.3)	(+0.4)	(+0.1)
Balance on current account	**−10.2**	**−10.7**	**−11.1**	**−7.6**	**−8.0**	**−10.5**	**−7.3**
Transfers from (+) and to (−)							
Lire clearing account of CGV	+0.6	+0.5	−0.8	−2.2	−1.0	+1.0	−0.9
Foreign exchange account of CGV	+0.6	—	−0.5	−0.2	+0.2	−0.7	−0.3
Foreign exchange holdings of CCMS	+0.4	+0.9	−0.4	+0.2	−0.5	−0.3	−0.7
Securities sold (+) and bought (−)	+0.2	—	—	—	−1.0	+1.4	+0.6
Other capital flows	+0.1	—	—	—	+0.8	+0.5	+0.2
Balance of capital	**+1.9**	**+1.4**	**−1.7**	**−2.2**	**−1.5**	**+1.9**	**−1.1**
Italian Government contributions	**+8.3**	**+9.3**	**+12.8**	**+9.8**	**+9.5**	**+8.6**	**+8.4**

Source: Annual Reports of the Italian Government to the United Nations on Somalia.

The Problem of Financial Dependence

TABLE 26

SOMALIA'S EXPORTS EXPRESSED AS A PERCENTAGE OF IMPORTS,
1895–1950

YEAR	Per Cent	YEAR	Per Cent
1895	100	1923	22
1896	103	1924	29
1897	77	1925	37
1898	54	1926	22
1899	—	1927	16
1900	—	1928	31
1901	—	1929	34
1902	—	1930	35
1903	—	1931	34
1904	83	1932	44
1905	76	1933	51
1906	49	1934	51
1907	56	1935	5
1908	57	1936	4
1909	40	1937	13
1910	47	1938	20
1911	36	1939	41
1912	34	1940	—
1913	26	1941	19
1914	29	1942	30
1915	33	1943	27
1916	36	1944	22
1917	64	1945	30
1918	42	1946	58
1919	54	1947	83
1920	46	1948	73
1921	17	1949	89
1922	22	1950	83

Sources: for 1895–1898, T. Carletti, *I Problemi del Benadir*, Viterbo, 1912; for 1904–1931, Ministero delle Colonie, *Statistica del Movimento Commerciale Marittimo dell'Eritrea, della Somalia Italiana, della Tripolitania e della Cirenaica;* for 1932–1934, G. Corni, *Somalia Italiana*, Milan, 1937; for 1937–1939, Governo della Somalia Italiana, *Relazione del Governatore per l'Anno XVII*, Mogadiscio, 1940; for 1935–1936 and 1941–1944, Four Power Commission of Investigation for the Former Italian Colonies, II, *Report on Somaliland*, London, 1948; for 1945–1948, Camera di Commercio, Industria e Agricoltura della Somalia, *Relazione del Consiglio Direttivo per l'Anno 1948–49*, Mogadiscio, 1949; for 1949 and 1950, U.N. Doc. T/1296. Figures for 1904–1913 refer to financial years, beginning July 1 of the year shown and ending June 30 of the following year.

not available for years prior to 1951, and the balance of trade, of course, is not the balance of payments. But since the balance of invisibles appears to be consistently passive for those years for which data are available, it does not seem unreasonable in this case to treat the balance of trade as representative of trends in the balance of payments on current account. In this respect it is interesting to note that in 1895 the balance of trade of Somalia was in equilibrium and in 1896 it even showed a slight surplus. But in those years Somalia did not exist as a political entity and there were no costs of central administration to be met. Moreover, external subsidies were not available then, and the volume of imports had therefore to be limited to what could be paid for with exports.

To put it another way, the fact that Somalia's balance of trade has been steadily passive since 1897 is largely accounted for by a high marginal propensity to import. In view of the size and importance of the subsistence sector in the Somali economy, domestic output tends to be highly inelastic and the variety of goods that consumers can obtain from it is narrowly circumscribed; consequently a rise in money incomes from whatever source tends to be translated into a higher demand for imported goods. The flow of foreign funds designed to maintain a level of government expenditures above that of domestic revenues thus also helps to maintain a level of imports and a standard of living in excess of the possibilities which the country's aggregate output alone can afford. A definite relation can therefore be said to exist between the deficit in the public budget and that in the balance of trade.

As Table 27 shows, consumer goods represent on the average about three-fifths of all imports, food products and textiles alone accounting for almost two-fifths. The high proportion of consumer goods is explained chiefly by two factors. One is the transfer of labor and other productive agents from the subsistence to the market sector of the economy. To the extent that this has occurred, subsistence output has declined, thereby forcing a rise in imports of food and other necessities. The other factor is the presence of the Italian population, whose consumer demand cannot be satisfied to any significant extent by domestic output,

The Problem of Financial Dependence

TABLE 27

THE COMPOSITION OF IMPORTS AND EXPORTS
(*Millions of U.S. $ Equivalents*)

ITEM	1951	1952	1953	1954	1955	1956	1957
IMPORTS (c.i.f.)							
Food products	3.8	3.4	2.8	2.7	2.9	2.9	2.2
Textiles	3.1	3.1	2.1	2.0	2.1	2.0	2.4
Other consumer goods	2.6	2.5	2.2	2.2	2.7	2.9	3.2
Capital goods	1.8	2.5	1.7	1.8	2.9	4.3	4.9
Fuel	1.1	1.3	1.1	1.3	1.4	1.8	1.0
Raw materials and semi-manufactures	0.9	1.9	1.0	1.5	2.1	2.2	2.7
Total	13.3	14.7	10.9	11.5	14.1	16.1	16.4
EXPORTS (f.o.b.)							
Bananas	5.2	6.2	5.7	6.6	8.0	5.7	6.4
Cotton	0.7	2.0	0.6	0.3	0.2	0.7	0.2
Hides and skins	1.1	0.8	0.9	0.8	1.2	1.1	0.9
All other	1.0	1.4	1.4	1.5	2.0	3.4	3.2
Total	8.0	10.4	8.6	9.2	11.4	10.9	10.7

Source: Annual Reports of the Italian Government to the United Nations on Somalia. For 1951–1955 export figures have been adjusted to show actual f.o.b. values for banana and total exports on the basis of data cited in U.N. Doc. T/1296, and for later years on the basis of information furnished by the banana producers' associations in Somalia.

largely because of differences in taste between Italians and Africans and in part also because of the insufficiency of domestic output. In recent years imports of consumer goods have tended to decline slightly; this tendency can be attributed almost entirely to the decrease in the number of Italians living in Somalia, many of whom have, for one reason or another, left the country since the inception of trusteeship.

It may be asked at this point whether devaluation of Somali currency would not help to bring about an equilibrium in the country's foreign trade. The answer is that devaluation is not likely to be effective because of the dominant role of bananas, which on the average account for about 60 per cent of the value of all exported goods. As has been explained in Chapter V, transport forms a large proportion of the cost of banana exports and must be paid for in foreign currency; hence devaluation would affect exports adversely and thus offset any gain that might be derived from a decrease in the volume of imports.

It is easy to understand, therefore, why AFIS does not expect a rapid improvement in the balance of trade in the years immediately following the establishment of the independent state of Somalia. It does, on the other hand, look forward to an improvement in the balance of invisibles, owing to an expected increase in the inflow of foreign investment funds by private companies engaged in the search for oil. On this basis, it has calculated that the deficit in the balance of payments may be reduced to five million dollars by 1962, that is, to an amount equal to the estimated deficit in the public budget for the same year.[4] These estimates may be somewhat too optimistic; even so they are significant, for they tend to underscore the lack of any fundamental solution to the problem of financial dependence which may continue to plague Somalia long after it has become an independent state.

THE BANANA TRADE AND ITALIAN SUBSIDIES

STATISTICS SHOWING the margin of disequilibrium in the balance of payments do not fully measure the extent of external aid that Somalia requires in the form of subsidies. These statistics measure the deficit only in so far as exports and other earnings are not able to pay for imports of commodities and various services. But since exports consist mainly of bananas sold in Italy at prices above those prevailing on the world market, note must be taken of the fact that an additional subsidy is provided indirectly through the protection that the Italian Government accords the Somali banana industry. For it is not difficult to realize that if banana exports were to cease altogether and were not replaced by other goods, the deficit in the balance of pay-

[4] AFIS, *op. cit.*

ments would grow considerably larger. According to AFIS calculations, cessation of the banana trade would increase the deficit by about two-and-a-half million dollars. This figure is arrived at by subtracting from the loss of banana sales the value of imports no longer required by the banana industry, and by taking into account the decreases in personal remittances abroad and in the outflow of capital revenue that could be expected to follow. The deficit in the public budget would also grow by another one-and-a-half million dollars.[5] These estimates, it must be observed, are perhaps too conservative. They do not take into account the negative multiplier effects that inevitably would be felt in Somalia if the activities of the banana industry were suddenly discontinued. Nevertheless they are useful, in that they emphasize the importance of the banana industry as an instrument of Italian support to Somalia.

It is in this connection that the role of AMB, the Italian banana monopoly, appears to be particularly significant. AMB, it may be recalled, is called upon to perform three major functions: first, it must guarantee a profitable market for Somali bananas; second, it must limit the quantity and fix the retail price of bananas sold in Italy so as to allay the fears of Italian citrus producers about alleged dangers of substitution; third, it must provide revenues for the Italian Treasury. With regard to the first two functions, it was pointed out earlier that there would be ample justification for dispensing with AMB. For the fears of citrus producers do not appear to be well founded, and protection for the Somali banana industry could be afforded more cheaply and just as effectively through a preferential tariff. The fact that AMB is also used as a fiscal instrument, however, adds an element of complexity to the issue that must be considered carefully.

The fiscal feature of the organization of the banana trade ap-

[5] *Ibid.*

pears in the price paid by the Italian wholesale distributor. This price includes the profit of AMB, but since AMB is a government agency, the profit is actually a tax, the ultimate burden of which falls upon the Italian consumer. The proceeds of the tax are turned over to the Italian Treasury and thus help to finance subsidies for Somalia. Should AMB be dropped, the Italian Government could make up for the loss of funds without reducing subsidies to Somalia only by raising other taxes, by resorting to deficit financing, or by reducing public expenditures. From the point of view of the Italian Government, some of these alternatives may be economically disadvantageous, and all of them may be politically inconvenient.

Malagodi has suggested that by setting up a preferential tariff of a particular type it would be possible to abolish AMB, give the Somali banana industry the degree of protection it requires, lower retail prices of bananas for Italian consumers, and at the same time raise even larger revenues for the Italian Treasury. The preferential tariff he has in mind would consist of two margins: a protectionist margin, which would be imposed upon bananas of non-Somali origin, and a fiscal margin, which would fall upon all bananas imported into Italy. Wholesale and retail banana prices would thus be able to fluctuate and on the average could be expected to fall; but the fall in prices would be accompanied by a higher volume of consumption in Italy, and the Treasury would therefore benefit through larger tariff revenues.[6]

There is much to be said in favor of Malagodi's proposal. Nevertheless the Italian Government may feel that there are certain political disadvantages to it, compared with the retention of present arrangements. Economic analysis can offer no guide regarding the political implications of the banana trade between Somalia and Italy. Ultimately, then, the question whether

[6] G. F. Malagodi, *Linee Programmatiche per lo Sviluppo Economico e Sociale della Somalia*, Rome, 1953, pp. 107–108.

AMB should be dissolved or not must be decided on the basis of political value-judgment, and only the Government of Italy is competent to make a decision of this kind. There can be no doubt that to Italy AMB is a cost, but so long as Italy must provide subsidies for Somalia, this cost simply represents the price paid for the political conveniences that AMB affords to the Italian Government.

In view of the close connection between Italian subsidies for Somalia and the banana trade, it is astonishing to find the World Bank Mission to Somalia recommending abandonment of banana production. The Mission bases its case primarily upon the argument that the banana industry is uneconomic. It finds it "difficult to believe," the Mission states in its report, "that the long-run interests of Somalia would be served best by keeping indefinitely in existence an industry which is uneconomic."[7] At the same time the Mission admits that there are no export crops, at least in the foreseeable future, that could take the place of bananas. "Bananas offer the highest returns of any crop under Somalia conditions," the Mission writes, "and while physical conditions and the ability of the Italian farmers would undoubtedly make it possible to raise other export crops successfully . . . none of them is believed to be a practical alternative as the basis for a concession economy."[8] Nevertheless, the Mission believes that banana production should be given up, though it recognizes that such action would require an increase in direct subsidies to Somalia. For without such an increase "there would be a drastic reduction in present standards of administration, education and the social services, the abandonment of much of the pioneer work already carried out and the frustration of hopes for higher living standards in the future."[9]

[7] U.N. Doc. T/1296, p. 93.
[8] *Ibid.*
[9] *Ibid.*, p. 91.

In the light of the circumstances presented, the Mission's argument that the banana industry is uneconomic indicates a certain amount of confusion. The statement that a particular activity is "uneconomic" is usually taken to mean that the resources devoted to it could be more profitably employed elsewhere. But the Mission admits that any alternative employment of the resources used by the banana industry would be less profitable. Actually, what seems to preoccupy the Mission is the uncompetitiveness of Somali bananas on the world market. The Mission is extremely pessimistic regarding the Somali banana industry's chances of achieving a competitive position in the future.

> Notwithstanding the labor, technical skill and capital that have been lavished on the concessions, the banana industry has been unable to overcome its competitive disadvantages. It has demanded, and so far received, special treatment. Even if the industry were reorganized in the generally more favorable conditions along the Giuba, conditions as to soil and climate and above all transport would still be superior in other exporting countries.[10]

One cannot deny that there is considerable justification for the pessimistic sentiments voiced by the Mission. But the evidence that the Somali banana industry could under no circumstances become competitive in the future is by no means conclusive. Of course, if Italy should suddenly decide to give no further protection to banana producers, the industry in Somalia would die. But if Italy should, on the other hand, decide to abolish AMB and replace it with a system of gradually declining preferential tariffs, for a relatively limited period of time, it is possible that the industry might yet achieve an economically tenable position. For under these circumstances powerful incentives would be created for the establishment of a more efficient organization of production and distribution.

[10] *Ibid.*, p. 92.

The Problem of Financial Dependence

The fact that the banana industry is a means by which Italy subsidizes Somalia makes these considerations appear to be largely irrelevant, however. Not only would Somalia fail to gain anything from the cessation of banana production, but there is a good chance that it would actually suffer a net loss, even if compensation for the loss of banana revenues were provided through additional direct subsidies; for cessation of banana production would in all probability cause unfavorable psychological repercussions on other economic activities, actual and potential. The chief problem facing Somalia is how to secure a politically independent existence for itself without external subsidies. Abandonment of the banana industry does not solve this problem.

It may be argued that abandonment of the industry would at least benefit the Italian consumer, since Italy would then turn to cheaper sources of supply. The argument holds only on the assumption that some other nation, or nations, would assume the subsidy burden now borne by Italy. Otherwise the position of the Italian consumer would remain unaffected, since gains derived from the lower cost of imports would be transferred to Somalia.

In the final analysis, then, the question whether the Somali banana industry should continue to function or not depends upon who is to provide subsidies for Somalia in the future. There is at present no indication that the subsidy burden now shouldered by Italy will be shifted to somebody else, and so long as this is the case there does not appear to be any substantial reason why the weak and fragile economy of Somalia should be administered so rude a blow as abandonment of the banana industry would undoubtedly entail.

THE ROLE OF MONETARY POLICY

THE PROBLEM posed by chronic deficits in the balance of payments is further complicated by foreign exchange difficulties, particularly in respect of sterling. As may be seen in Table 28, the balance of payments on current account shows, apart from a small dollar surplus, large lire and sterling deficits. The deficit with Italy, accounted for by invisibles, causes no particular foreign exchange problem because Italian grants are made available

TABLE 28

BALANCE OF PAYMENTS ON CURRENT ACCOUNT BY MONETARY AREAS
(*Millions of U.S. $ Equivalents*)

	LIRE		
YEAR	Commodities	Invisibles	Balance
1951	+0.2	−4.4	−4.2
1952	+1.9	−6.9	−5.0
1953	+1.9	−8.6	−6.7
1954	+2.0	−6.2	−4.2
1955	+2.2	−6.2	−4.0
1956	+0.7	−7.7	−7.0
1957	+0.9	−5.9	−5.0

	STERLING				DOLLARS		
YEAR	Commodities	Invisibles	Balance		Commodities	Invisibles	Balance
1951	−5.6	−0.5	−6.1		+0.1	n	+0.1
1952	−5.4	−0.2	−5.6		−0.1	n	−0.1
1953	−4.4	−0.4	−4.8		+0.2	+0.2	+0.4
1954	−4.1	+0.1	−4.0		+0.3	+0.3	+0.6
1955	−5.0	n	−5.0		+0.4	+0.6	+1.0
1956	−5.1	n	−5.1		+0.6	+1.0	+1.6
1957	−4.2	n	−4.2		+0.4	+1.5	+1.9

Source: Annual Reports of the Italian Government to the United Nations on Somalia.
n = negligible.

in lire. A problem does arise, however, in connection with the sterling deficit, which is due to the fact that a very substantial proportion of Somalia's imports comes from British Somaliland, Aden, Kenya, and other sterling zone territories, whereas most of its exports go to Italy.

In an attempt to cope with this situation, imports from the sterling zone during the trusteeship period were at first restricted

The Problem of Financial Dependence

by means of license regulations, but gradually these restrictions were relaxed. A few items still require an import license, which is usually granted if evidence can be produced to show that the importation of these items from Italy would cost considerably more than their importation from the sterling zone.[11] A certain amount of pressure is thus applied to reorient trade toward Italy, even though this tends to raise the cost of imports; all the same, goods originating from the sterling-zone continue to form a high proportion of total imports (Table 29).

TABLE 29

IMPORTS BY MONETARY AREAS
(*Per Cent*)

YEAR	LIRE	STERLING	DOLLARS
1951	50.3	48.8	0.9
1952	52.3	46.8	0.9
1953	48.5	51.5	—
1954	55.5	44.5	—
1955	52.5	45.0	2.5
1956	48.8	49.6	1.6
1957	51.0	47.4	1.6

Source: Annual Reports of the Italian Government to the United Nations on Somalia.

Up to now, deficits with the sterling zone have been met by using lire and the small dollar balances to purchase sterling. To explain the monetary mechanism employed for this purpose, it is necessary to give a brief description of the functions of the Cassa per la Circolazione Monetaria della Somalia (CCMS) and of the Mogadiscio branch of the Banca d'Italia, the two institutions primarily responsible for monetary policy in Somalia under the trusteeship.

CCMS is a note-issuing institution, located in Rome. It was created at the time the trusteeship was established, when it was decided to introduce a new currency in Somalia. As was noted

[11] See U.N. Doc. T/1296, pp. 64–65.

earlier, the currency which had circulated officially there since 1925 had been the lira, but during the Second World War, when the territory fell under British military occupation, the East African shilling replaced the lira; and when the trusteeship régime was set up it was deemed inadvisable to reintroduce Italian money, and a new monetary unit, the somalo, was created instead. The somalo has a gold parity of 0.124414 grams. It is equal in value to the East African shilling and equivalent to U.S. $0.14. Present regulations call for a 100 per cent cover of gold, silver, or foreign exchange, with the exception of denominations smaller than one somalo, for which no cover whatever is required.

A major task of CCMS, in addition to its purely passive functions as a note-issuing institution, is the repurchase of Somali currency in territories adjacent to Somalia but within the sterling zone. Repurchase is made necessary by the fact that a considerable volume of traffic usually streams to and from Somalia in border regions where it is nearly impossible to exercise any kind of monetary control. If the somalo were not acceptable in adjacent sterling territories, its general acceptability within the country itself would be impaired. Every year, therefore, CCMS repurchases—through the facilities of Barclays Bank (D.C. & O.) and of the National Bank of India and after payment of a small commission—all Somali currency that may find its way to Nairobi, Mombasa, Zanzibar, Aden, and other sterling-zone markets (Table 30).

Central banking functions are performed by the Mogadiscio branch of the Banca d'Italia. In principle, these include control of the reserves of all commercial banks operating in Somalia. The Somali Credit Institute is required, under existing regulations, to hold as a reserve against demand deposits an amount equal to 20 per cent of the excess of such deposits over the Institute's capital. The other commercial banks are branches of Italian credit institutions, and each of them is required by Italian law to main-

TABLE 30
REPURCHASE OF SOMALOS BY CCMS

YEAR	Thousands of U.S. $ Equivalents	As % of Imports from the Sterling Zone	As % of Total Imports
1951	783	*12.5*	*6.1*
1952	806	*13.0*	*6.5*
1953	539	*11.0*	*5.6*
1954	711	*16.4*	*7.3*
1955	1,210	*22.8*	*10.3*
1956	1,742	*27.7*	*13.7*

Source: Cassa per la Circolazione Monetaria della Somalia (communication to the author).

tain a reserve equal to 40 per cent of the excess of demand deposits over an amount ten times as large as the bank's capital. In practice, there is little scope for regulation of the domestic money supply. The total supply of money is small and a relatively high percentage of it is in currency (Table 31). This is not surprising, in view of the relatively small size of the market sector of the economy. Moreover, commercial banks are usually in a highly liquid position and, with the exception of the Somali Credit Institute, can always count on the resources of parent offices in Italy to meet any additional liquidity needs that may arise.

TABLE 31
THE SUPPLY OF MONEY IN SOMALIA

As OF DECEMBER 31	MILLIONS OF U.S. $ EQUIVALENTS			CURRENCY AS % OF TOTAL MONEY SUPPLY
	Currency in Circulation	Demand Deposits	Total Money Supply	
1951	4.8	3.6	8.4	57.2
1952	3.7	4.8	8.5	43.6
1953	3.8	5.1	8.9	42.7
1954	4.0	5.8	9.8	40.9
1955	4.6	6.7	11.3	40.8
1956	4.7	6.3	11.0	42.8
1957	5.4	6.9	12.3	43.9

Sources: Cassa per la Circolazione Monetaria della Somalia and Banca d'Italia of Mogadiscio (communication to the author). Figures for demand deposits refer to net amounts and exclude interbank deposits.

163

The most important control functions of the Banca d'Italia concern foreign exchange transactions. These are handled through a special account known as Conto Gestione Valutaria (CGV), which consists of two sections, one for settlement of accounts in lire through clearing arrangements which are maintained both in Italy and in Somalia, and the other for settlement of accounts in other foreign currencies. Through CGV, the Banca d'Italia meets the sterling deficit by purchasing sterling with lire, and to some extent with dollars, either from Italy's Foreign Exchange Office or from CCMS.[12] To the extent that the Banca d'Italia purchases sterling from CCMS—and it usually does so only as a last resort—corresponding changes take place in the composition of the note cover (Table 32).

TABLE 32

COMPOSITION OF THE NOTE COVER

(*Per Cent*)

As of December 31	Lire	Dollars	Sterling	Gold
1951	41.1	6.7	52.2	—
1952	27.9	8.3	63.8	—
1953	32.4	8.8	58.7	0.1
1954	13.6	23.9	62.4	0.1
1955	50.6	30.5	18.8	0.1
1956	52.0	29.5	18.4	0.1

Source: Cassa per la Circolazione Monetaria della Somalia (communication to the author).

The end of the trusteeship régime in 1960 will obviously necessitate a change in monetary institutions. With respect to CCMS no particular problem need arise, since CCMS can be easily transferred to Somalia. Some other agency, however, will have to assume the functions currently performed by the Banca d'Italia. It has been vaguely suggested that the Somali Credit Institute should assume those functions. But the Institute may find it ex-

[12] U.N. Doc. T/1296, pp. 104–107.

ceedingly difficult to separate central banking from its other functions and may become the victim of various political pressures. It would seem advisable, therefore, to create a separate central bank. But no matter how this question is actually going to be resolved, it is fairly evident that monetary policy in Somalia will have to continue to be closely integrated with monetary policy in Italy.

THE CONCEPT OF FINANCIAL DEPENDENCE

THE PROBLEM of Somalia's financial dependence, as it is called here, refers to the fact that chronic deficits in the budget and in the balance of payments bar the road to the achievement of genuine political independence. There is a widespread tendency to regard this problem as an extreme manifestation of a wider phenomenon embracing the African continent and probably all underdeveloped countries. This phenomenon is the lack of self-sufficiency, which is alleged to give rise to particularly acute difficulties because of the absence of diversification in production.

Historically, the idea that concentration in a few lines of production for export is inherently evil appears to be a relic of the world depression of the thirties. For it was widely believed then that concentration in a few lines of production had been instrumental in preventing underdeveloped countries from insulating themselves against the effects of the depression as it spread from the United States. Strangely, perhaps, the advocates of diversification seemed to overlook the fact that countries with highly developed and diversified economies had also failed to stem the tide of depression. At any rate, economic insulation is obviously not the answer to the problem of world depression. The best defense seems to lie in international economic co-operation and in the adoption of appropriate domestic policies for the swift restoration of full employment by the country responsible for generating a sharp cyclical downswing.

Analytically, it is necessary to ask why underdeveloped countries have tended to concentrate in a few lines of production. The answer to this question is simple: given the structural characteristics of an underdeveloped economy, concentration in a few lines of production yields the greatest return to investment within a relatively short time. Generally speaking, therefore, deliberate diversification will result in an uneconomic allocation of resources. Only on the assumption that the world market price for the exported commodity, or commodities, is determined under monopsony conditions would it perhaps be possible to build a tenable theoretical case in favor of deliberate diversification, though even in this case some doubt might be entertained. In the real world, at all events, the instances where this assumption holds true are comparatively rare.

Diversification need not be viewed, however, as the result of a deliberate effort. It may also be conceived of as the natural consequence, so to speak, of a high degree of economic development. If so, the problem of diversification is merely synonymous with the problem of economic development, and no special significance can be attached to it.

While not much can be said in favor of the argument for diversification, even less can be said in favor of the argument for self-sufficiency, if self-sufficiency is understood to mean autarchy. Few, if any, countries can afford to pursue autarchic policies, and Somalia would be inviting disaster if it attempted to do so.

But autarchy is only one of several meanings which the term "self-sufficiency" may take on. The ambiguity of the term raises an issue of a certain importance in the case of Somalia, because under the terms of Article 3 of the trusteeship agreement covering that territory Italy obligated itself, among other things, to "promote the economic advancement and self-sufficiency of the inhabitants"; [13] the agreement, however, provides no clue as to what should be understood by "self-sufficiency" and the nature of the obligation assumed by Italy in connection with it, in the light of conditions as they exist in Somalia.

The term "self-sufficiency" appears frequently in discussions relating to economic policy in British East Africa. There it is usually taken to mean that the subsistence requirements of the indigenous population should be met, in so far as possible, out of domestic output. What such a policy is supposed to accomplish is not altogether clear. The reasoning behind it seems to be that, inasmuch as the economic growth of an underdeveloped economy depends in a substantial measure upon capital, encouragement of self-sufficiency in subsistence goods would tend to promote such growth through its effect on the composition of imports; for to the extent that its achievement would reduce the need for consumer-good imports, room would be made for a larger inflow of capital goods from abroad. In contrast to autarchy, self-sufficiency in this sense does not imply a withdrawal from international trade.

But the argument for a policy of self-sufficiency in native subsistence goods neglects the repercussions that such a policy might have upon export trade. Assuming that imported subsistence goods cost less than the same goods produced locally, a shift from imports to domestic output would raise production costs in export industries. The resulting contraction in the volume of exports might offset, and perhaps even more than offset, the increase in capital-good imports which the fall in consumer-good imports alone would permit. In considering the effect of a policy of self-sufficiency in native subsistence goods upon capital imports it is necessary to take into account the entire foreign trade picture and the factors that influence it, not merely the composition of imports. In any event, it is hard to see why self-sufficiency in this sense should be actively encouraged in Somalia. For there, as

[13] U.N. Doc. T/Agreement/10.

we have seen, most imported subsistence goods compare unfavorably in cost with those produced locally. To pursue a policy of self-sufficiency under these circumstances would be superfluous, since the price mechanism is already exerting strong pressure in favor of domestic production of native subsistence requirements.

Self-sufficiency may also refer to the ability of a country to conduct its economic affairs without having to depend upon external subsidies. In this case it is perhaps more appropriate to speak of financial self-sufficiency. For a brief spell at the end of the nineteenth century, financial self-sufficiency formed one of the cardinal principles of economic policy in British dependencies. The enunciation of the principle has been attributed to Earl Grey.[14]

It is this last-mentioned concept which seems to have the greatest relevance to conditions in Somalia, though it is necessary to reformulate it along somewhat narrower lines. For there appears to be no justification for the view that Somalia should not take advantage of any foreign grant capital that might be offered to finance public expenditures for the country's development. Should the new state of Somalia fail to obtain foreign grant capital for this purpose, the future prosperity of the country's inhabitants might be impaired, but the new state would at least be able to maintain itself. A different problem arises, however, when, as is the case at present, the government must also resort to foreign subsidies in order to meet ordinary public expenditures.

What this means is that the real problem in Somalia is not dependence on foreign trade, a condition common to most countries in the world, but one-sided dependence. If a country such as England, which is heavily dependent on foreign trade for its standard of living, were suddenly cut off from channels of international economic intercourse, it would doubtless be worse off

[14] A. Pim, *The Financial and Economic History of the African Tropical Territories,* Oxford, 1940, p. 175.

as a result, but so would the rest of the world; whereas if Somalia were cut off from international trade, it would be worse off, but the rest of the world would not. In other words, the condition of financial dependence indicates lack of interdependence, not of self-sufficiency in the sense of autarchy. The solution of this problem lies not in withdrawal from, but in more effective participation in, international trade.

Obviously, such a solution is possible only through additional economic development. Note must be taken of the fact, however, that there is an inherent conflict between a policy of economic development and one aiming at the elimination of financial dependence. For the basic objective of economic development is a rise in the standard of consumption, and if all gains from increased efficiency in production were used to reduce deficits in the public budget and in the balance of payments—as was done, for example, in 1956, when gains in SAIS production of sugar were absorbed by the government through higher taxes, thereby leaving the domestic retail price unchanged [15]—incentives for development would be reduced. If this is to be avoided, economic and fiscal policy in Somalia will have to steer a careful middle course.

[15] U.N. Doc. T/1311, pp. 78–79.

[CHAPTER IX]

The Significance of the Experiment in Somalia

———— ⟨✧⟩ ————

JULY 1, 1960, will mark the date on which Somalia will cease to be a politically dependent territory and take its place in the community of nations as a fully sovereign member.[1] It will also be a day that will see a somewhat strange, awkward, and inherently dangerous divorce take place between formal political institutions and economic realities. For at that time, and for many years to come, the country will still be in the same condition of financial dependence in which it has found itself ever since it was organized as a single political unit. Genuine independence will not have been achieved, since the new state of Somalia will not be able to function without external subsidies. The country's economy has never been, and is not now, strong enough to carry

[1] Somalia was originally scheduled to receive its independence on December 2, 1960, but by a resolution adopted on December 5, 1959, the General Assembly of the United Nations advanced the date by five months.

the financial burdens of central administration. The basic reason for this, as the foregoing analysis has endeavored to show, is structural. During the period of trusteeship Somalia has received a considerable amount of capital aid, but this aid, though in many ways beneficial, has not modified the country's economic structure. Nor was it intended to. Nor was it indeed possible to carry out such a tremendously difficult task within the short space of ten years. As an experiment in the feasibility of meeting nationalist aspirations in dependent areas by setting time limits for independence, trusteeship in Somalia must therefore be adjudged a failure. Of this fact, now that the trusteeship régime is almost at an end, there can no longer be any doubt.

It would be a pity, however, if the failure of the experiment, instead of inducing sober reflection about its significance and a new resolve to search for more realistic ways of coping with the tasks that lie ahead, were to give rise to a purely emotional reaction. There is a real danger that the facile, almost reckless, optimism which pervaded the earlier discussions and proposals that eventually led to the experiment will now give way to an extreme and equally unjustified pessimism. For the view may come to prevail that Somalia's problem of financial dependence is wholly insoluble. Already some voices have been heard urging the United Nations to put off indefinitely the date on which it is to grant independence to Somalia. Such a course of action, were it embarked upon, would almost certainly give rise to much political instability in Somalia without in any way contributing to the solution of a single economic problem. Fortunately, its advocates are few and the United Nations has shown no disposition to heed their advice. But the pessimistic mood which may come to predominate as a result of the experiment's failure may cause the international community to withhold external support to the extent and in the form in which it will be most vitally needed. This is not to say that the need for subsidies will be ignored, at least in the near future. It is also to be expected that a fair measure of technical assistance and some capital assistance will continue to be provided. What may not be realized is that, if the problem of financial dependence is to be solved, it will be necessary to pursue an appropriate economic policy; and that in this respect the international community will still have to discharge an important responsibility, despite the transformation of Somalia into a sovereign state.

AN ECONOMIC POLICY FOR SOMALIA

THERE ARE those, in and out of Somalia, who believe that the problem of financial dependence is simply a matter of taxes. In their view the Somali Government, once independence is achieved, could take a long step toward a solution by instituting additional taxes, which the Italian Administration either did not dare, for fear of incurring popular hostility, or did not see fit, for a variety of reasons, to impose during the trusteeship régime. This view ignores the relation between per capita income and ability to pay taxes; the fact is that per capita income in Somalia is far too low to permit a sizable increase in government revenues. The first point to be stressed, therefore, is that a realistic economic policy aiming at an eventual solution of the problem of financial dependence must be based on a clear recognition of the fact that hopes for a solution hinge on the possibility of increasing per capita income.

Apart from possible oil discoveries—which may have a beneficial effect on the country's economy, although, as pointed out earlier, this is far from certain—the greatest hope for future development seems to lie in the exportation of new crops. For the country's agricultural potentialities have by no means been exhausted. What opportunities the production and export of grapefruit, papaya, and various vegetable fibers may have to offer, for example, are still largely undetermined, yet worth exploring. Under these circumstances it seems logical that a serious effort should be made to step up technical research and experimentation and to encourage small-scale commercial ventures designed, among other things, to test the reaction of foreign demand and the feasibility of using production methods which reflect as closely as possible existing relative factor scarcities in the country.

Technical research and commercial exploration imply a trial-and-error procedure hardly compatible with the rigidities inherent in comprehensive planning. Comprehensive planning is in any event not feasible in Somalia, since, as we have seen, even the most elementary statistical data needed for this purpose are lacking. The situation in Somalia thus requires that investment continue to be governed by a highly decentralized process of decision-making; under these conditions a major task of government policy will be to prevent any inconsistencies from arising between public and private economic activities. It will be particularly important, if development is to be fostered, to prevent public capital from being so used as to maintain or strengthen subsistence activities; to make adequate provision not only for maintenance but also for replacement of public capital facilities; and to devise fiscal measures which will take account of the need for reducing dependence on foreign subsidies as well as of the need for maintaining incentives to increase output and productivity.

What is thus implied with respect to Somalia's future economic development is that, should it occur at all, it is likely to do so through a gradual and evolutionary, but not necessarily harmonious, process. For the results of technical research and commercial exploration cannot be foreseen; the very nature of such endeavors suggests that one may expect many failures and setbacks to precede the achievement of even a measure of success, if indeed any will be achieved at all. But the economy of Somalia is obviously too weak to withstand many violent shocks. For this reason it is of the utmost importance that early and careful consideration be given to the situation which prevails with regard to the banana trade; for if steps are taken to put the banana trade on a sound economic basis, it may yet provide a comfortable cushion with which to absorb the impact of experimentation in other fields of production and economic organization. Obviously, however, this will require action in spheres which lie wholly outside the control of the Somali Government. The successful implementation of economic policy in Somalia will thus depend upon a large measure of international co-operation, without which the independence that the United Nations has decided to grant to that country will be tantamount to international dereliction.

ECONOMIC FACTORS AND POLITICAL CHANGE

BUT WE MUST still consider the wider implications of the Somali experiment. As was pointed out in the first chapter, political change in Africa is currently being viewed in terms which suggest an underlying assumption that politics and economics represent independent spheres of social activity. The experience of Somalia under the trusteeship clearly indicates that this assumption is not valid.

It will perhaps be objected that this argument is based on a single case; that Africa is a large continent characterized by an extreme diversity of conditions; and that neither Somalia nor any other single territory can be regarded as representative of it. This, of course, is true. It may even be added that many African countries, though not all, are probably more fortunate than Somalia in that they are at least able to meet the ordinary costs of central administration without having to depend on foreign aid. But while true, this is beside the point. For the proposition that economic factors are not relevant to political change is usually presented as valid a priori, and to disprove such a proposition one case is sufficient. What the Somali experience teaches is not that political change in Africa is an impossibility because of economic factors, but that if genuine political change is to be brought about, it is necessary, among other things, to take into account the role of economic forces, though this role may be different, of course, in each individual case.

The significance of trusteeship in Somalia, however, is not limited to the fact that in the initial decision to set a time limit for independence economic factors were completely ignored. It was inevitable that sooner or later, once the trusteeship régime was established, one would have to come to grips with the territory's economic difficulties. What is particularly noteworthy is the basic philosophy which permeated all suggestions and every attempt to cope with them. For the decision to transform Somalia into a sovereign state within ten years was a political decision, that is, an act of the human will; the subsequent realization that powerful economic obstacles stood in the way of carrying out this decision led to a search for ways and means by which political power, that is, human volition, could be used to remove them. But the failure of the Somali experiment was not a failure of the human will; it came about through the operation of impersonal forces.

The Somali experiment thus shows that political power alone cannot be counted upon to solve economic problems. Nor is there any reason to believe that more can be accomplished by going to the other extreme, that is, by adopting an attitude of complete *laissez-faire*. It would seem, then, that some kind of a compromise must be achieved. This, however, should not be understood as a reference to the concept of "mixed economy," even though it suggests a middle ground. For the "mixed economy" is a purely quantitative concept, and therefore inadequate; by itself it does not explain which functions can be most efficiently performed by the government and which should be left to the mechanism of the market. What is needed for this purpose is a clarification of the relation of politics to economics.

This was realized long ago by the Austrian economist Böhm-Bawerk, after he became involved, at the end of the nineteenth century, in a bitter and protracted controversy between the German Historical School and the Austrian School of economics. To students of the history of economic doctrine, this controversy is known as the *Methodenstreit*. The debate centered around the question as to whether politics should have primacy over economics, as contended by the Historical School, or whether, as the other side maintained, economics should have primacy over politics. Böhm-Bawerk reached certain conclusions which shed much light on the nature of the main problem discussed in this book. They were published in a relatively little-known article shortly before the outbreak of World War I.

According to Böhm-Bawerk, the attainment of economic objectives, contrary to what the Historical School had contended, does not depend entirely upon the human will, of which the State is the most powerful expression. Nor does it, despite the arguments presented by the Austrian School, depend entirely upon objective economic forces, since economic laws do not have the characteristics of natural laws. The participants in the *Methodenstreit*, Böhm-Bawerk believed, debated a false issue. What was important was to understand the nature of economic laws and their effect upon political power. Economic laws are logical laws; as such they set limits to political power, though within these limits political power can be used to advantage. Economic laws, for instance, allow ample scope for resort to political power to change the distribution of personal income; on the other hand they leave very little room for its use in changing the distribution of returns to factors of production. The limits may therefore vary, depending upon the specific characteristics of individual economic laws. Böhm-Bawerk concluded that political power has an important role to play, but if the limits set by economic laws are transgressed, recourse to it will prove to be futile.[2]

The failure to understand the nature of economic laws and their relation to political power is precisely what has tended to plague most recent discussions about Africa's economic problems. What is generally understood is that the kind of political change now witnessed in Africa creates an "urgent need" to solve certain economic problems and that political power can, and should, be used to that end. It is seldom realized, however, that economic forces are governed by laws (or principles) and that political power can be used effectively only within the limits set by those laws. It cannot, therefore, be assumed that it will always be possible to alter economic conditions in the way and with the rapidity which the course of political events seems to demand. Therein lies the most significant lesson to be learned from the experiment in Somalia.

[2] E. Böhm-Bawerk, "Macht oder Ökonomisches Gesetz?" *Zeitschrift für Volkswirtschaft, Sozialpolitik und Verwaltung,* XXIII (1914), Vienna.

APPENDIX

A Note on Some Implications of the European Common Market

THE ANALYSIS of Somalia's fundamental economic characteristics and problems presented in the text of this book takes no account of the impact which the European Common Market may have on that country's economy. Neglect of this important issue has been justified by the fact that the European Common Market was formed only recently, that it has not yet acquired a definitive shape, and that it is, therefore, still too early to obtain a clear view of its implications. Nevertheless, the creation of the European Common Market is too important an event to be passed over in complete silence. Consequently, this brief note is appended.

The European Common Market came into being on January 1, 1958, following the conclusion of the Rome Treaty on March 25, 1957. It is essentially a program for the gradual elimination of all tariffs and other artificial barriers to trade and factor mobility among six European member states: France, Germany, Italy, Belgium, the Netherlands, and Luxemburg. The Rome Treaty, however, also provides for the association of overseas countries and territories with which the member states may have special relations. Several African countries, including Somalia, have thus been linked with the Common Market.

Two things should first of all be noted. One is that the Common Market does not represent a step toward the liberalization of world trade. Its major aim is regional economic integration, and under present world conditions this implies the necessity of erecting powerful economic barriers so as to prevent possible interferences from the outside. The other is that the European Common Market appears to be largely a misnomer; for, as currently conceived, it may be said to be a Eurafrican rather than a European scheme.

To what extent Somalia can be expected to benefit from inclusion in the Common Market is far from clear. Under the provisions of the Rome Treaty, a Development Fund has been set up to aid the associated countries, but this does not mean that Somalia will therefore be able to receive capital assistance from European countries other than Italy. During the period 1958–1962, Somalia is scheduled to receive a total equivalent to five million dollars from the Development Fund, while Italy's contribution to the Fund is about eight times that amount.

More significant than any capital aid may be the changes in international trade patterns that are bound to follow the establishment of the Common Market. Banana producers in Somalia are particularly likely to be affected by them. Up to now their chief potential competitors on the Italian market have been producers in the Canary Islands and in Guinea. The Common Market can be expected to maintain the tariff barriers erected by Italy against bananas of Spanish origin, since Spain is not a member. As for Guinea, it is to be noted that since 1956 the price of bananas originating from that country has risen to a point where it compares unfavorably with the price of those from Somalia.[1] The explanation is to be found partly in higher production cost and partly in improved French demand.[2] It is not yet possible to tell, however, whether the current price disadvantage of Guinea bananas in comparison with those from Somalia represents a new long-term trend or merely a temporary phenomenon. Moreover, Guinea's decision to leave the Franco-African Community and to become an independent state has created a new element of uncertainty concerning that country's economic relations with the Common Market.

Another important consideration is that the basic principles underlying the Common Market are hard to reconcile with the continued existence of institutions such as AMB. Italy may therefore be induced to suppress the banana monopoly and to replace it with provisional protectionist measures designed to permit the Somali banana industry to adapt itself to free market conditions. It is of course not possible to predict whether the Somali banana industry will actually be able to survive under these conditions. On the other hand, the pessimistic views expressed in this respect on the basis of past performance should not be regarded as conclusive. The only sure method of determining whether the Somali banana industry can compete in a free market is to allow it to do so.

[1] See U.N. Doc. T/1372, pp. 45–46.
[2] Ministère de la France d'Outre-Mer, *Bulletin de Conjoncture des Territoires d'Outre-Mer,* No. 14 (December, 1957), pp. 13–14.

Index

Abgal, the, 63n
Africa: contrast with Asia, 10
Agriculture: irrigated, 79–83, 87–88, 95, 104, 107, 125, 134; rain-fed, 79–80, 81–83, 104
Ahrens, T. P., 66n
Amministrazione Fiduciaria Italiana della Somalia (AFIS), 26, 27, 82n, 123, 126, 127, 128, 130, 131, 136, 139n, 141n, 148–49, 154, 155
Anonima Cooperativa Coltivatori Afgoi (ACCA), 87–91
Anthropologists: role in African studies, 10–11; and cattle-complex theory, 52–63
Anticolonialism, v, 2–10
Asians, in Somalia, 22–23
Austrian School of economics, 176–77
Autarchy. See Self-sufficiency.
Authoritarianism: in Africa, 7

Autochthones, 22
Azienda Monopolio Banane (AMB), 90–94, 95, 98–99, 102–104, 155–58, 180

Bananas, 32, 43–44, 87–104, 111–12, 120, 133, 153–59, 174, 179–80; as substitutes for citrus fruits, 95–98, 102, 155; export quotas, 94; Italian demand for, 90–91, 95–98, 102; overproduction, 95, 98, 100; uncompetitiveness of Somali producers, 90, 92, 99–100, 102–103, 158; undervaluation of exports, 46–47
Banca d'Italia, 161, 162–64
Barclays Bank, 162
Bartolozzi, E., 75n
Batten, T. R., 54n, 77n
Bauer, P. T., 55n
Becker, G. H., Jr., 14n

Bettini, T. M., 51n, 74n
Bigi, F., 104–105n
Boeke, J. H., 116–17
Böhm-Bawerk, E. E., vi, 176–77
Bozzi, L., 49n, 66n
Brand, W., 4n
Bride-price, 50, 51n, 52, 56, 57, 58, 59, 70
Bross, H., 84n
Brotto, E., 23n
Brusa, A., 101n

Capital, 52, 73, 86, 158; allocation of, in Seven Year Plan, 133–35; as substitute for labor, 83, 105, 107–10, 120–21; demand for, 70–71, 78, 94; of Somali Credit Institute, 140; revenue, in balance of payments, 149
Capital assistance, 129, 170–71, 172, 179
Capital equipment, need for replacement of, 138–39, 173
Carletti, T., 118n
Caroselli, F. S., 119n
Casilli d'Aragona, M., 43–44n
Cassa per la Circolazione Monetaria della Somalia (CCMS), 161–62, 163, 164
Cavallini, G., 99n
Cavendish, 89
Central bank, functions of, 162–65
Cibelli, E., 100n, 101n
Colombo, M., 44n
Commercial banks, 85, 162–63
Commodity flows, intersectoral, 113–17
Communications: in Seven Year Plan, 125–26, 133–34
Comparative advantage, theory of, 121–22
Compulsory destocking, 72
Conforti, E., 81n, 82n, 100
Conspicuous waste, 54, 56
Conto Gestione Valutaria (CGV), 164

Co-participation, 105
Corfitzen, W. E., 51n, 75n, 124n, 135n
Corni, G., 151
Cortinois, A., 50n, 74n
Cost of transfer, 76–77, 93–94, 95, 99, 100–101, 121, 134, 144–45
Costanzo, G. A., 22n
Cryptogamic diseases, 89
Cufino, L., 74n
Currency: changes in, 44–46, 161–62; share of money supply, 163. See also Money.

Deficits: in balance of payments, 12, 146, 149ff.; in public budget, 12, 146–49, 152, 155, 165, 169; of ENAM and Somali Credit Institute, 143
Desheks, 80–82
Devaluation, 153–54
Development Fund, 179
Di Lauro, R., 69n
Dual economy, 31, 36, 39, 114–17, 122, 145
Durra, 32, 81
Dussert, E., 96n

East Africa Royal Commission, 73n, 77n
Economic calculation, 33, 59, 116
Economic crisis at Afgoi, 88
Economic laws, 176–77
Economic surplus, 59–63
Economic planning: central, 6–10, 131–32; in Africa, 7–8; in Somalia, 16, 19–37, 123–40, 173
Education, role of, in economic development, 137
Efficiency, technical and economic, 69–70
Einaudi Law, 140–41
El Marashly, M. S., 105n
Ente Nazionale Ammassi e Motoaratura (ENAM), 143–44
Evans-Pritchard, E. E., 55n

Factor proportions, 119–120, 173
Factor transfers, intersectoral, 113–17, 134, 145, 152
Fantoli, A., 66n
Fars, 80–81
Ferretti, U., 74n
Ferro-Luzzi, G., 49n
Festa, A., 44n
Fioresi, L., 100
Fletcher School of Law and Diplomacy, v
Folco, A., 69n
Food and Agriculture Organization (F.A.O.), 49n, 97
Foreign exchange: changes in rates, 44–46; control, 46; difficulties with sterling zone, 159–65; necessity of, for repayment of loans, 118; requirements of SAIS, 111–12; theory of, 45
Four-Power Commission of Investigation for the Former Italian Colonies, 16n, 151
Francolini, B., 99n, 100n
Frankel, S. H., 6

Germann, R. F., 83n
Gilal, 69
Goldenweiser, A., 53n
Gorini, M. P., 51n
Grain: stockpiling program, 141–44; underground storage of, 83–84
Grey, Earl, 168
Gros Michel, 89
Grottanelli, V. L., 119n
Gulliver, P. H., 54n, 58n

Haberler, G., 115
Haile Selassie, 13
Halm, G. N., v
Harris, M., 62n
Hemorrhagic septicaemia, 68
Henry, Y., 100n
Herskovits, M. J., 57–63

Historical School of Economics, 56, 176
Hoof-and-mouth disease, 68, 74–75

Independence: nominal versus real, 16; time limits for, 11, 13, 170–71, 175
Interdependence: in international trade, 168–69
Interest rates: charged by petty traders, 84–86; of Somali Credit Institute, 140–41
International Cooperation Administration (ICA), 124, 126, 130–31, 134–36
International Monetary Fund, 46
Investment: basic aspects of, 137–38, 140; foreign, 102, 107, 110–11, 117–18, 144, 154; public, 126, 132–33, 137, 173; private, 126–27, 132, 138
Istituto Agronomico per l'Oltremare, v
Istituto Centrale di Statistica, 23, 24, 25, 26, 27, 30
Italian colonies, disposition of, 13–15
Italo-Ethiopian conflict, 12–13, 43

Jie, the, 54
Jouve, P., 96n
Juba nana, 89

Karamajong, the, 52
Kenya Land Commission, 54n, 72n
Kenya-Uganda Railway, 135
Keynes, J. M., 70
Kindleberger, C. P., 98n
Kinzy, G., 51n, 75n
Klemme, M., 71n

Labor: backward-bending supply curve, 119; scarcity of, 82–83, 86, 94, 99, 104–10, 114–15, 117ff.
Land: relative abundance of, 120; suitability of, for use, 31–32; utilization of, 32

Lessona, A., 118n
Lewis, I. M., 23n, 27n, 49n, 50n
Lewis, W. A., 55n, 137
Liquidity-preference, 70
Lusini, G., 44n

McColloch, C. L., 75n, 76n
Maffi, Q., v
Mainardi, G., 52
Malagodi, G. F., 34–35, 93n, 95n, 124, 156
Mallarini, A., 74n
Malthusian checks, on livestock, 71–72
Mangano, G., 119n
Mangano, P. A., 14n
Marginal propensity to import, 152
Marshall, A., 137
Martoglio, F., 74n
Masai, the, 52
Maugini, A., 41n, 69n, 77n
Maximum program, 125–26
Meregazzi, R., 107n
Methodenstreit, 176
Minimum program, 125–26
Mixed economy, 175–76
Money: livestock as, 59; prices, 115–17; total supply of, 163
Monopoly power: of AMB, 91; of RAMB, 101
Monopsony power: of AMB, 91, 103–104; of SAIS, 108; and diversification, 166
Multiplier effect, 155
Musa sapientum. See Gros Michel.
Musa sinensis. See Cavendish.
Musson, A. L., 69n

National Bank of India, 162
Natural resources, conservation of, 72–73; relative value of, 33–34; role of, 38, 144
Noli, C., 106
Nomadism, 24–25, 29–30, 36, 66, 136
Nuer, the, 52, 54–55

Ogaden, the, 51n
Oil, expectations concerning, 132, 144–45, 172
Onor, R., 63n, 85n
Opportunity costs, 29, 36–37

Panama disease, 89
Paoletti, A., 99
Pastoralism, 24–25, 31–34, 38ff., 82–83, 114–15, 136, 138–39
Pearson, H. W., 62n
Pigou, A. C., 137n
Pim, A., 168n
Pleuropneumonia, 68
Polanyi, K., 62n
Politics: different meanings of the term, 8; relation of, to economics, 1–18, 20, 139–40, 174–77
Port facilities, 76, 94, 121, 125–26, 135
Prestige system, 57–58
Priorities in Seven Year Plan, 124
Production: diversification of, 165–66; roundabout method of, 115–17; vertical structure of, 115–16
Production functions, changes in, 73–75
Public works, 133

Rava, M., 119n
Reciprocal demand, 122
Regia Azienda Monopolio Banane (RAMB), 101–102
Reinicke, F. G., 126n
Ricardo, D., 60
Rinderpest, 68, 74–75
Rivlin, B., 14n
Roads, 29–30, 94, 121, 125–26, 135
Rocchetti, G., 43n, 44n, 88n, 89n, 91n, 93n, 94n, 95n
Rome Treaty, 178–79

Sakellaridis, 104
Salt, exports to Japan, 44n
Schneider, H. K., 54n
Schumpeter, J. A., 73

Self-sufficiency: as autarchy, 101, 166, 169; financial, 168; in subsistence goods, 84, 167–68
Seminomadism. *See* Nomadism.
Shamba tax, 148
Sikatoga disease, 89
Social science, analytical categories in, 2
Società Agricola Italo-Somala (SAIS), 106–12, 130, 169
Società Agricoltori Giuba (SAG), 87–90, 130, 140
Società Anonima Cooperativa Agricola di Genale (SACA), 87–91, 130, 140
Somali Credit Institute (*Credito Somalo*), 125, 130, 140–44, 162–65
Somalia: early Italian influence in, 11–12; independence date for, 13, 170; size of, 29; use of name, 11n
Somalia Development Fund, 130–31
Somalo, 45, 162
Statistical parameters, 19
Statistics, basic, 20–21, 36, 173
Subsidies, 12, 102, 129–31, 143, 147, 152, 154ff., 170–73
Subsistence concept: in cattle-complex theory, 60, 62; in Ricardian theory, 60

Tariffs: on bananas, 91, 100, 155, 156, 158; on sugar, 110; under European Common Market, 178ff.
Taxation, attitude toward, 30–31, 36, 148

Taxes, 138, 169, 172; indirect, 148; user, 76n
Technical assistance, 124, 131n, 149, 172
Tonga, the, 52
Totalitarianism, African rejection of, 7
Tozzi, R., 82n
Transhumance, 69
Transport facilities, 76, 94, 121, 125–26, 133ff., 144–45
Triulzi, G. A., 49n, 66n
Trypanosomiasis, 68, 69, 79
Turkana, the, 54

Underpopulation, 118–19
United Nations Advisory Council, 15
United Nations missions to Somalia, 9, 16, 20–21, 55–57, 128

Van Dyke, A. S., 126n
Veblen, T., 56

Wages, at SAIS, 107–10
Wainhouse, D. A., 14n
Water: development of supplies, 125; scarcity of, 64–67, 71–72
Watussi, the, 52
Wells, 64, 71, 125, 130, 134
Westermann, D., 10n
Work, attitude toward, 50, 68–69, 108
World Bank Mission, 16, 47–48, 93, 145, 149, 157–58
Worzella, W. W., 69n

Yamey, B. S., 55n